The Culinary Guide for MSPI

Written by
Jane E. Wise

The Culinary Guide for MSPI

Written by
Jane E. Wise

First Edition

Design and layout by Curious Design, Inc., Huron, OH
Printed in the U.S.A. by PrintOne Digital, Cleveland, OH

ISBN 0-9764023-0-0

Table of Contents

Foreword

Disclaimer
Dedication
Acknowledgement
Author's Story
Author's Notes

Product Information

Ingredients to Avoid
Product List for Infants and Toddlers
Product List for Children and Adults

Recipes

Resources

 Denotes a kids-voted favorite

Disclaimer

The Culinary Guide for MSPI offers recipes and information for general educational purposes only. Endorsement is not issued by the companies listed nor is this information intended as substitute for advice, recommendation or treatment from a health care professional. Recipes, product lists and other information found in this cookbook are not exhaustive nor do they cover all treatment for MSPI. It is important to follow the advice from a health care professional regarding health care needs.

Dedication

To my husband Eric, thank you for all of
your love and support.

To my two children Megan and Pieter, thank you
for bringing so much love and joy into my life.

Acknowledgement

First, I want to thank Pieter's pediatrician, Dr. Amy Carruthers for diagnosing Pieter with MSPI. I want to thank my editors: my husband Eric and my parents for proofreading and critiquing this cookbook. To my Thursday play group who always took into consideration our dietary needs when hosting lunch. Thank you to my mother-in-law, Mary, who along with me learned how to cook without dairy and soy and became educated on reading food labels. To all my family and friends who are a constant source of encouragement.

Our son Pieter, a healthy 9.8 lb baby was born on January 28, 2003. During the first few weeks Pieter developed a dry itchy rash (atopic eczema) on his face, arms and legs, he cried constantly and would projectile vomit. I took Pieter to his pediatrician and during his check up he provided the doctor with a stool sample. The stool had traces of blood and a spinach like look to it (green and leafy). Tests were performed which indicated Pieter to be intolerant to milk and soy proteins – MSPI (milk soy protein intolerant).

MSPI is a condition when an infant can not digest the proteins found in milk and soy foods. Even infants who are solely breastfed can develop the symptoms from maternal ingestion of cow's milk (which then passes into the breast milk). Each time the mother or child comes into contact with a form of milk and/or soy protein the infant will exhibit unpleasant symptoms. MSPI usually causes these symptoms within the first month of life.

Board certified allergist Dr. Albert H. Cobb explains that a food intolerance or sensitivity in a newborn is due to IgG antibodies traversing the placenta in utero. For example, the placenta of cattle has six layers that protect the embryo from food antibodies in the mother. The calf gets protective immunoglobulins from the colostrum in the milk at birth. In contrast, the human placenta has only one layer, so maternal antibodies pass through rather easily; the baby will hiccup when the mother eats offending food. The colostrum in her milk is less important to immunize the baby. When dealing with food problems in the newborn or young child, we ask "What did the mother crave or eat a lot of when she was pregnant?" Often, the same food that the mother craved or overate during pregnancy is the cause of the baby's problem.[1]

A child with MSPI may cry 18 hours or more a day. Symptoms may manifest in the skin, digestive system or the respiratory system. MSPI babies retch repeatedly and projectile vomit. They may have chronic congestion and diarrhea, blood or mucus in their stool and/or green leafy stool that looks like spinach leaves. The small intestine, colon, or both may be affected. MSPI babies may refuse feedings because their stomach hurts or conversely, want to eat all the time because they feel temporarily better just after feeding.[2] MSPI is more severe than colic. Colic does not extend past three months of age and colicky babies cry intermittently, usually for a couple of hours at the same time each day.

Currently, there are no medications that cure MSPI, nor is there a way to prevent MSPI from developing. However, there are two ways to avoid a reaction:

1. Breastfeed. Both the mother and child must eliminate all milk and/or soy protein foods from their diets.

2. Formula. Purchase any of the three hydrolyzed protein formulas, Nutramigen, Alimentum or Pregestimil. A 1 lb. (16 oz.) can costs between $22.00 and $29.00, lasting about 7 days. It is important to note that the formulas may not be covered by insurance companies because they are not deemed a health necessity.

MSPI is a growing problem with 2 - 7% of babies under one year being affected; it is the most common form of food allergy.[3] If not treated properly, MSPI can pose serious health risks. Babies with severe cases can lose weight, develop more slowly, suffer internal bleeding and extensive inflammation in their intestinal tract; they may even be hospitalized for intravenous feeding.[4] What is such a great concern is that normal methods of soothing a baby with MSPI (such as rocking, swaying and/or pushing them in a stroller) will not work. Therefore doctors and parents speculate that parents without support may lose control, resulting in MSPI babies being exposed to shaken baby syndrome.

Progress is being made. With strict attention to both baby and mothers' dietary needs it is possible for babys' with MSPI to eat foods with milk and soy protein. 95% of those who follow a milk and soy protein free diet do outgrow MSPI and begin transition to regular milk and solid foods by age one year.[5] More still needs to be done to prevent MSPI in babies. The cause can not be fully explained. Many pediatricians are trained where MSPI is not recognized, thus may miss the diagnosis. Parents may not know what is normal and hesitate to call their pediatrician or a specialist. Research needs to continue and parents need to be aware of the symptoms. This is an ongoing collaborative effort among parents, pediatricians and researchers.

I chose to change my diet and continue breastfeeding. After three weeks we saw a distinct difference in Pieter. The crying stopped, the rashes went away and his stool became a normal healthy color. Today, Pieter can eat foods that contain both milk and soy protein.

Eliminating milk protein and/or soy protein from ones diet is a cooking adventure in itself. After spending several hours in the grocery store reading ingredient labels I wondered how many others were doing the same. Whether you are cooking for yourself, a family member, or a friend, The Culinary Guide for MSPI is designed to take the guesswork out of cooking. In each recipe, brand name products that do not contain milk and soy protein are listed making grocery shopping hassle free. I wanted to be sure that each dish is easy to prepare and enjoyed by the entire family thus all recipes have been tested and approved by my family and friends. Please watch for the kids-voted favorites throughout the cookbook.

Enjoy the cooking adventure!

Jane E. Wise

Jane E. Wise

- Products are item, not brand specific for example: Fleischmann's® Unsalted butter/margarine does not contain milk protein or soy protein, however, Fleischmann's® Regular butter/margarine does. Swanson's® 99% fat free chicken broth contains soy protein but Swanson's 100% fat free chicken broth does not.

- Product lists and recipes exclude both milk and soy protein. Some children may be allergic to milk protein and not to soy protein. Cook accordingly.

- Milk is one of the easiest ingredients to substitute in baking and cooking. Milk can be replaced, in equal amounts, with water, rice milk or fruit juice. For example, use 1 cup of water in place of 1 cup of milk.

- Food allergy and food intolerance are often mistaken for one another. While they may share similar symptoms, food allergy is an immune system response while food intolerance occurs when another system of the body (usually the digestive tract) reacts adversely to a food.[6]

- To prevent high risk children, such as those with MSPI, from developing a food allergy, eliminate milk and dairy products from diet until the child is 1 year old. Avoid introducing eggs (especially egg whites) until he is 2 years old, and peanuts, tree nuts and fish until he is 3 years old.[7]

- Lactose intolerance is different from milk protein intolerance. Lactose intolerance is the inability to digest significant amounts of lactose, the predominant sugar of milk.[8] Milk protein intolerance is the inability to digest the proteins found in cow's milk.

- Possible hidden sources of milk:
  - Deli meat slicers are frequently used for both meat and cheese products.
  - Some brands of canned tuna fish contain casein, a milk protein.
  - Many non-dairy products contain casein, a milk derivative.
  - Some meats may contain casein as a binder.
  - Many restaurants put butter on meats, such as steak, after they have been grilled to add extra flavor. The butter is not visible after it melts. It is important to discuss your order with the waiter or manager.[9]

Ingredients to Avoid

It is important to avoid foods that contain any of the following ingredients. A glossary of ingredients with an (*) are listed on page 117.

Milk Protein

- artificial butter flavor
- butter, butter fat, butter oil, butter milk
- casein*
- caseinates (ammonium, calcium, magnesium, potassium, sodium)*
- cheese
- cottage cheese
- curd*
- custard*
- Ghee*
- Half & Half®
- hydrolysates (casein, milk protein, protein, whey, whey protein)*
- lactalbumin, lactalbumin phosphate*
- lactoglobulin*
- lactose*
- lactulose
- milk
- nougat
- pudding
- rennin casein
- sour cream
- sour milk solids
- whey*
- yogurt

Following items MAY contain milk protein:

- flavorings including: caramel, bavarian cream, coconut cream, brown sugar, butter, and natural chocolate
- Natural flavoring (some products indicate dairy as part of the natural flavoring ingredient)
- high protein flour
- margarine
- Simplesse®

Ingredients to Avoid

Soy Protein

- hydrolyzed soy protein
- miso*
- shoyu sauce*
- soy (albumin, flour, grits, nuts, milk, sprouts)
- soybean (granules, curd)
- soy protein (concentrate, isolate)*
- soy sauce
- tamari*
- tempeh*
- tectured vegetable protein (TVP)
- tofu*

Following items MAY contain soy protein:

- hydrolyzed plant protein
- hydrolyzed vegetable protein
- natural flavoring
- vegetable broth
- vegetable gum
- vegetable starch

Note:
1. Soy lecithin is listed on many food products. Soy lecithin is safe to consume, it is a substance commonly used in foods which are high in fats and oils in order to make dissimilar substances, such as oil and water, blend and/or stay blended.[10]

2. The following terms may be misconstrued. Note that they do not contain milk protein and do not need to be restricted.[11]
    a. calcium lactate
    b. calcium stearoyl lactylate
    c. cocoa butter (refers to the meat of the cocoa bean)
    d. cream of tartar
    e. lactic acid (lactic acid starter culture may contain milk)
    f. oleoresin
    g. sodium lactate
    h. sodium stearoyl lactylate

Product Information

As part of the public health mission to keep food safe, the U. S. Food and Drug Administration (FDA) is increasing its activity on food allergen awareness. FDA's 2001 allergen priorities for the Center for Food Safety and Applied Nutrition (CFSAN) describe new initiatives. For example; a major goal is to provide guidance to industry and regulators on how to manage allergens through appropriate manufacturing and labeling practices.[12]

The
Culinary Guide
for MSPI

Product List for Infants and Toddlers

Listed in this section are name brand foods that do not contain milk and soy protein in the product. This is not a comprehensive list of products. The list is compiled in alphabetical order by product with name brands below. For more information on food labeling visit: www.cfsan.fda.gov/~dms/alrgawar.html.

Baby/Toddler Foods ~ Stage 1 and Stage 2

- Earth's Best® Organic Biscuits
  - Wheat- Free Teething Biscuits

- Gerber® Graduates® Turkey Stew, Chicken Stew and Vegetable Stew with Beef

- Gerber® Cereal
  - Single Grain Rice
  - Single Grain Oatmeal Regular
  - Single Grain Oatmeal Regular with Bananas

- Gerber® Finger Foods™
  - Fruit Wagon Wheels

- Gerber® Graduates® Lil 'Entrées
  - Chicken Noodle Dinner with Oatmeal, Pears and Cinnamon
  - Chicken Stew with Noodles and Green Bean Dices
  - Pasta Wheel Pick-Ups and Chicken with Carrot Dices
  - Turkey and Green Bean Dices with Sweet Potatoes

- Gerber® Graduates® for Toddlers – snacks
  - Apple Graham Crisps
  - Banana or Vanilla Cereal Snackin' Squares
  - Fruit Juice Snacks
  - Veggie Crackers

- Nature's Goodness™ Turkey Rice Dinner – Stage 2

- Nature's Goodness™ Vegetable Turkey Dinner – Stage 2

Product List for Infants and Toddlers

Baby/ Toddler Foods ~ Stage 3

- Beech Nut Naturals®
  - Sweet Potatoes
- Chiquita® Bananas

- Beech Nut Naturals™
  - Spaghetti and Beef Dinner
  - Country Vegetable and Chicken
  - Tender Chicken and Stars
  - Turkey Rice Dinner

Product List for Children and Adults

Bacon
- Louis Rich® Turkey Bacon
- Oscar Mayer® Low Sodium Bacon

Bagels
- Thomas'® New York Style Bagels – multi grain

Beans
- Brook's® Chili Beans
- Bush's® Best Original Baked Beans
- Campbell's® Pork and Beans
- Casa Fiesta® Refried Beans

Biscuits
- Giant Eagle® Biscuits Home-Style

Breads
- Brownberry® white sandwich buns
- Country Hearth® Deli Rye with caraway seeds
- Delections® Sun-dried Tomato Basil Flat-out Bread
- French bread
- Millbrook® Cleveland Rye
- Millbrook® Honey and Wheat bread
- Pocket-Less Pita® Traditional White
- Roman Meal® 100% Whole Grain bread
- Schwebel's™ Kaiser rolls with or without sesame seeds
- Schwebel's™ Old World Flat Bread – white, Italian herb or wheat
- Father Sams™ regular white or wheat pocket bread

Bread crumbs
- None

Broth / Bullion cubes/ Stock
- Herbox® chicken and beef bullion cubes
- Kitchen's Best® vegetable and chicken stocks
- Kitchen Basics® Natural Seafood Stock
- Knorr® chicken, beef and fish bullion cubes
- McCormick® Bouillon Cubes, chicken flavored
- Swanson's®100% fat free Chicken Broth
- Swanson's® 99% and 100% fat free Beef Broth

Product List for Children and Adults

Brownies
- Duncan Hines® Chocolate Lover's Brownies Double Fudge
- Duncan Hines® Family-Style Brownies Chewy Fudge
- Tops® Chewy Fudge Deluxe Brownie Mix (Sold at Tops® grocery stores)

Butter/Margarine
- Fleischmann's® unsalted or light butter/margarine sticks

Candy
- Swedish Fish, gummy bears
- Licorice, red and black

Note: Hard candies such as caramels, toffees, peanut brittle contain a milk protein.

Cake mixes
- Duncan Hines® Moist Deluxe® classic yellow, Devil's food, orange supreme, strawberry supreme, pineapple

Cereal - good for snacking
- Cheerios®
- Cap'n Crunch®

Cheese
- None

Chocolate chips
- Sam's Choice™ Real Semi-Sweet Chocolate chocolate chips (Sold at Sams' Club™ and Wal-Mart®)
- Tops® Semi-Sweet Chocolate Chips (Sold at Tops® grocery stores)

Cocoa
- Hershey's® European style Dutch Processed Cocoa
- Hershey's® Unsweetened Cocoa

Coffee
- Ground/whole bean coffees

Note: Products such as Cappuccino, Latte's, Frothé®, International Coffee's® contain Whey.

Coffee cream
- None

Product List for Children and Adults

Cookies
- Vista® Family Size Duplex Creams
- Vista® Family Size Assorted Creams
- Vista® Vanilla Wafers

Condiments
- French's® Classic Yellow Mustard
- Grey Poupon® Dijon Mustard made with white wine
- Heinz® Tomato Ketchup
- Kraft® Light Mayo
- Kraft® Miracle Whip Dressing
- Kraft® Mayo Real Mayonnaise

Corn syrup
- Karo® Corn Syrup

Crackers
- Honeymaid® Honey Grahams
- Nabisco® Original Premium Saltine Crackers
- Nabisco® Original Graham
- Triscuit® - original, low sodium and garden herb
- Wheat Thins® - low sodium, multigrain and original
- Zesta® Original Saltine Crackers

Crabmeat
- Bumble Bee® Fancy Lump Crabmeat
- Bumble Bee® Pink Crabmeat
- Chicken of the Sea® Crabmeat

Eggs
- Fresh eggs
- Egg Beaters® 99% Real Eggs
- Pappetti Foods® All Whites®

Flour
- Giant Eagle® bread flour and all-purpose flour (Sold at Giant Eagle® grocery stores)
- King Aruthur's® bread flour and all- purpose flour
- Pillsbury® bread and all-purpose flours
- Pillsbury® Softasilk® cake flour

Product List for Children and Adults

Frosting
- Duncan Hines® Creamy Home-Style Classic Chocolate
- Duncan Hines® Creamy Home-Style Classic Vanilla

Frozen desserts
- Edy's® Fruit Flavored Popsicles
- Luigi's® Italian Ice

Fruits
- Fresh and canned fruits including jams/jellies

Gravy
- Heinz® Home-Style Savory Beef Gravy
Note: Chicken gravy contains Whey.

Meats, fresh
- All fresh meats

Meats, packaged – see also sausage
- All Natural® Wellshire Farms™ Polska Kelbasa
- Bob Evans® Italian Sausage
- Johnsonville® Beer 'n Bratwurst®
- Johnsonville® Irish O' Garlic sausage
- Johnsonville® Italian Sausage – Hot

Milk
- Rice Dream® Rice Drink original and vanilla flavor

Muffins
- Duncan Hines® Bakery-Style Muffins Wild Maine Blueberry

Pancake/Waffle mix
- None

Pasta
- Dried boxed pasta
Note: Some frozen pastas such as ravioli or stuffed tortellini contain cheese filling.

Peanut butter
- Berkley & Jenson™ (Sold at B.J.'s® Wholesale Club stores)
- Giant Eagle® Peanut Butter creamy and crunchy style (Sold at Giant Eagle® grocery stores)

Product List for Children and Adults

Pie
- Marie Callenders® Dutch Apple Pie
- Marie Callenders® Raspberry Pie

Pie crust
- Giant Eagle® Pie Crust (Sold at Giant Eagle® grocery stores)
- Pillsbury® Pie Crust

Pop-corn
- Act II® Kettle Corn
- Food Club® Popping Corn, natural flavor
- Healthy Choice® Microwave Popcorn, natural flavor

Potato chips/Pretzels
- Fritos® Original Corn Chips
- Fritos® Scoops
- Lays® Classic
- Lays® Wavy Original
- Ruffles® Original
- Sun Chips® Original
- Rold Gold® Honey Wheat Braided Twists
- Snyder's® of Hanover Rods

Rice
- Kraft® Minute® Brown Rice
- Kraft® Minute® White Rice
- Zataran's® New Orleans Style Black Beans and Rice

Salad dressing
- Kraft® Light Done Right® Creamy French Style
- Wishbone® Russian Dressing

Sausage
- Bob Evans® Savory Sage Sausage
- Johnsonville® Original Recipe Sausage Links
- Johnsonville® Vermont Maple Syrup Breakfast Sausage Links

Product List for Children and Adults

Sauces
- Applesauce
- Barilla® Mushroom and Garlic
- Heinz® Chili Sauce
- KC Masterpiece® Hickory Brown Sugar Barbecue Sauce
- Open Pit® Grill Classics™ Original Barbecue Sauce
- Prego® Tomato, Onion and Garlic

Note: Some pasta sauces contain cheese, milk or soy product.

Seasoning
- Good Season®
- Lipton® Savory Herb with Garlic Soup and Dip Mix
- McCormick® Chili Seasoning

Shortening
- Crisco®
- Mrs. Tucker's®

Note: Some shortenings include an artificial butter flavor; artificial butter flavor is a milk protein.

Soups
- Campbell's® Bean with Bacon
- Campbell's® Tomato Soup

Note: cream soups contain a milk protein; most chicken noodle soups contain soy protein.

Tacos/Tortillas
- Old El Paso® Flour Tortillas
- Old El Paso® Taco Shells
- Ortega® Taco Shells

Note: Taco seasoning contains Whey.

Tuna
- Bumble Bee® Solid White Albacore - in water

Vegetables
- Fresh and canned vegetables

Yeast
- All packet and jarred yeast

Yogurt
- None

Intolerance to cows' milk protein is a type of intolerance that is common in babies and children. Symptoms start from the time when cows' milk is first introduced into the diet. There is no cure for it and the only way to stop the symptoms is to avoid cows' milk products.

The
Culinary Guide
for MSPI

Cocktails and Appetizers

The Culinary Guide for MSPI

Cocktails and Appetizers

Non-Alcoholic Cocktails

Classic Alcoholic Cocktails

Appetizers

Non-Alcoholic Cocktails

Iced Strawberry Tea

Servings: 2

Ingredients
2 1/2 c. hot water
5 Tbsp. Nestea® Iced Tea Mix with
    Sugar and Lemon
1/4 c. strawberry preserves
4 iced cubes
2 lemon slices

Instructions
Combine water, tea and preserves in a one-quart pitcher. Refrigerate for at least 2 hours; strain before serving. Serve each glass with a lemon slice.

Pink Smoothie Deluxe

Servings: 4

Ingredients
2 c. frozen banana slices
1 1/2 c. frozen, unsweetened strawberries
1 c. ruby red grapefruit juice
1 c. orange juice
4 whole strawberries, garnish
4 orange slices, garnish

Instructions
Combine frozen fruit and juice in a blender, purée until very smooth. Serve in frosted glasses. Garnish each glass with a strawberry and an orange slice.

Maraschino Cherry Cooler

Servings: 1

Ingredients
3/4 c. sweetened cherry juice
1/2 c. sparkling water
1/8 tsp. pure vanilla extract
1 maraschino cherry with stem

Instructions
Fill tall, slender glass with ice. Add cherry juice, sparkling water and vanilla extract; stir well. Garnish with a cherry and enjoy.

Medieval Holiday Wassail
Servings: 16

Ingredients
1 gallon apple cider
1 c. lemon juice
1/2 c. sugar
1- 10-inch cinnamon stick
1/2 tsp. whole cloves
3 oranges, sliced
16 orange slices, garnish

Instructions
1. In a 6-quart pot, combine cider, lemon juice and sugar. Bring to a boil stirring to dissolve sugar.

2. For spice bag, place cinnamon and cloves in center of a clean kitchen towel. Tie closed with a piece of clean string.

3. Add spice bag and 3 sliced oranges to cider mixture. Reduce heat, cover and simmer gently for 30 minutes. Remove spice bag and oranges and discard. Serve cider in mugs. Float orange slices in each mug.

Prickly Pink Limeade
The distinct vibrant red color comes from the flesh of the prickly pears.
Servings: 4

Ingredients
1 c. prickly pear juice*
1/2 c. fresh key lime juice
1/2 c. sugar
2 c. sparkling water, chilled
1 lime, cut in wedges

Instructions
Place pear juice, lime juice and sugar in a jar with a tight-fitting lid and shake vigorously to dissolve sugar. Pour over ice into 4 tall glasses and top off with sparkling water. Garnish with a lime wedge and serve.

*To peel a prickly pear, hold in place with the tines of a fork while you slice off each end with a sharp knife. Cut a lengthwise slit down the fruit and peel skin off flesh in a rolling motion. Juice and strain through a fine sieve (to eliminate seeds) before proceeding with recipe.

Non-Alcoholic Cocktails

Summer Sangria

Servings: 8

Ingredients
3 c. grapefruit juice, chilled
1 1/2 c. white grape juice, chilled
1 orange, peeled and thinly sliced
1 c. strawberries, hulled and sliced
1 1/2 c. club soda, chilled

Instructions
Combine juices, orange slices and strawberries. Add club soda when ready to serve.

Banana Slush

Wow your guests with this fizzy ginger ale fruit treat.
Servings: 22

Ingredients
2 c. sugar
3 c. water
1- 32 oz. each can pineapple juice and
    can orange juice
2 bananas, mashed
1/4 c. lemon juice
1- 2 liters ginger ale

Instructions
Combine sugar and water in a large-saucepan; bring to a boil. Stir until sugar dissolves. Remove from heat; cool before serving.

Berry Melon Granita

Servings: 8

Ingredients
3 crenshaw melons, rind removed,
    seeded and cubed
1/4 c. sugar
3 Tbsp. lemon juice
8 strawberries
8 blackberries

Instructions
1. Combine melon, sugar and lemon juice in a blender, purée until smooth. Pour juice through a fine strainer into shallow freezable container and freeze for 1 hour.

2. Run a fork through ice to break up crystals. Freeze again for 1 hour and repeat fork process. Serve melon granite in a martini glass and garnish with 1 strawberry and 1 blackberry. (Berries can be placed on a toothpick or just float in glass).

Classic Alcoholic Cocktails

Cherry Mimosa

Servings: 6

Ingredients
1/8 c. Grand Marnier® or other
  orange-flavored liquor
2 Tbsp. sugar
1 bottle chilled champagne
1 c. cranberry juice, chilled
6 maraschino cherries

Instructions
Pour Grand Marnier® in a small bowl. Place sugar in saucer. Dip rims of champagne glasses first in Grand Marnier®, then in sugar. Fill each champagne glass with three parts champagne and one part cranberry juice and garnish with a maraschino cherry.

Gimlet

Servings: 2- 2 oz. glasses

Ingredients
4 oz. dry gin
2 oz. fresh lime juice
2 lime wedges

Instructions
Combine gin and lime juice in a shaker half-filled with crushed ice. Stir well and strain into cocktail glass. Garnish each glass with a lime wedge.

Bulldog

This highball is on the lighter side with a refreshing fruit twist.
Servings: 2

Ingredients
3 oz. dry gin
3 oz. orange juice
4 oz. ginger-ale
2 maraschino cherry
2 orange slices

Instructions
Fill Collins glass with ice. Pour in gin and orange juice. Top off with ginger ale and garnish each glass with a cherry and an orange slice.

Classic Alcoholic Cocktails

James Bond Martini

This martini is made just the way James Bond likes his, "shaken, not stirred".
Servings: 2

Ingredients
4 oz. dry gin, chilled
1 oz. dry vermouth, chilled
2 green olives

Instructions
Place crushed ice in cocktail shaker. Pour in gin then vermouth. Cover and shake until outside of shaker becomes cold. Strain into chilled martini glasses. Garnish with olives.

Frozen Lime Daiquiri

Servings: 2

Ingredients
6 oz. rum
3 Tbsp. lime juice
2 Tbsp. sugar
4 c. ice, crushed
2 sliced limes

Instructions
In a blender, crush ice. Add to blender rum, lime juice and sugar; blend for 1 minute. Pour into a goblet and garnish with a lime slice.

Sparkling Wine Punch

Servings: 5 quarts

Ingredients
3 bottles of white wine, chilled
48 oz. pineapple juice, chilled
1 bottle champagne, chilled
6 oz. frozen lemonade concentrate

Instructions
Combine all ingredients in a large punch bowl. Stir until frozen lemonade is dissolved. Serve cold.

Potato and Curried-Beef Samosas with Mango Chutney

To celebrate our birthdays, Eric and I usually go to an Indian restaurant. Samosas are always on our order. Now we can have them at home. Serve these samosas with Mango Chutney.
Servings: 8

Ingredients

1 Tbsp. vegetable oil
1 onion, diced
1 Tbsp. curry powder
1 tsp. cumin
1/2 lb. beef
1 tsp. salt
1 1/2 c. diced frozen hash-brown potatoes
1 c. frozen mixed vegetables
1 c. Kitchen's Best® Chicken stock or
    1 Knorr® Chicken bouillon cube to
    1 c. boiling water
1 pkg. Pillsbury® refrigerated pie crust

Instructions

1. In a skillet heat vegetable oil. Add onions, curry and cumin; cook until onions are transparent. Add beef and salt. Cook until beef is browned. Stir in potatoes, frozen vegetables and broth. Bring to a boil, reduce heat and simmer for 3 minutes. Let cool in skillet for 5 minutes.

2. Preheat oven to 400°F. Cut both pie crusts along fold lines to make 8 pieces. Moisten straight edge of 1 piece of crust with water and seal to make a cone shape. Fill with 1/8 of beef mixture. Moisten and seal remaining edges to make a triangular pocket. Place on a baking sheet. Repeat with each piece of pie crust. Bake for 20 minutes.

Homemade Meatballs

Top spaghetti with these meatballs for a flavorful pasta dish.
Servings: 24 meatballs

Ingredients

2 lbs. ground beef
1 egg, slightly beaten
1 tsp. nutmeg
1/8 tsp. ground cloves
1/2 c. (14 crackers) Nabisco® Original
    Premium saltine crackers, crushed very fine
dash cayenne pepper

Instructions

In a large mixing bowl, mix all ingredients well. Shape into 3/4-inch balls. Place meatballs on a cookie sheet. Bake in a 350°F oven for 20 minutes, or until juices are clear.

Appetizers

Angie's Classic Party Meatballs
Servings: 12

Ingredients
Homemade meatballs, page 6
1 c. Heinz® Chili Sauce
1 c. grape jelly

Instructions
1. Bake homemade meatballs in a 350°F oven for 20 minutes.

2. Meanwhile, in a small sauce pan combine chili sauce and jelly until jelly is melted. Place meatballs in a serving dish. Pour jelly mixture over meatballs; stir gently to coat. Serve hot.

Bacon Shrimp Wraps
A unique and delicious way to serve shrimp.
Servings: 20

Ingredients
20 strips Oscar Mayer® Low Sodium
    bacon, uncooked
2 bunches fresh basil
40 medium shrimp, peeled and
    de-veined (tails on)
1/8 tsp. salt
1/8 tsp. ground black pepper
4 lemons, cut into wedges

Instructions
1. Preheat broiler. Cut uncooked bacon strips in half widthwise. On a large cutting board lay bacon strips flat. Place basil leaf in middle of each piece of bacon. Place shrimp on top of basil and tail at right angle to bacon strip. Wrap bacon around shrimp and place seam side down on broiling pan; secure with toothpick. Sprinkle with salt and pepper.

2. Broil 4 - 5-inches from heat for 3 minutes. Turn over and broil another 3 minutes. Squeeze lemon juice over cooked shrimp just before serving.

Ham and Pineapple Party Kabobs
Servings: 20

Ingredients
1/4 c. Fleischmann's® Unsalted margarine
1/4 c. orange marmalade
1 Tbsp. brown mustard
1/4 tsp. cayenne pepper
20 oz. can pineapple chunks, drained
1 lb. cooked ham, cut into 3/4-inch cubes
8 oz. can water chestnuts, rinsed drained and halved
1 large red and green bell pepper, seeded and cut into 3/4 -inch squares
20- 6-inch bamboo skewers

Instructions
1. Preheat broiler. In a saucepan, combine margarine, marmalade, mustard and cayenne pepper. Heat on low until melted; mix well and set aside.

2. Alternate pineapple, ham, water chestnuts and bell peppers on skewers. Brush with reserved sauce and place on a shallow broiler pan. Place 4 - 5 inches from heat and broil for 4 - 5 minutes, turning occasionally; broil until browned on all sides. Serve immediately.

Elegant Crab Balls
Servings: 16

Ingredients
1 c. (28 crackers) Nabisco® Original Premium saltine crackers, crushed fine
3 Tbsp. sherry
1 Tbsp. lemon juice
1 Tbsp. onion, grated
1 tsp. dry mustard
1/2 tsp. salt
1/8 tsp. pepper
8 oz. BumbleBee® Fancy Lump Crabmeat, shredded
1/2 lb. Oscar Mayer® Low Sodium bacon, uncooked
1 package toothpick

Instructions
1. Preheat broiler. In a bowl combine crushed crackers, sherry, lemon juice, grated onion, dry mustard, salt and pepper. Stir in shredded crabmeat. Shape into 1-inch balls. Cut bacon strips in half and wrap around crab balls; securing each with a toothpick.

2. Place on broiler pan. Broil until bacon is crisp, about 10 minutes, turning to brown evenly.

Appetizers

Cajun - Style Chicken Nuggets

*The Cajun seasoning adds zip to these
chicken nuggets.*
Servings: 8

Ingredients
1/2 c. Ruffles® Original potato chips,
    finely crushed
1 1/2 tsp. chili powder
1 tsp. cumin
1 tsp. thyme
1/4 tsp. cayenne pepper
2 lb. boneless, skinless chicken breast,
    cut into 1-inch chunks
2 c. vegetable oil

Instructions
1. In a large bowl, combine crushed
potato chips, chili powder, cumin, thyme
and cayenne pepper. Dip chicken breast
pieces in crumb mixture; coating well.
Set aside.

2. In a large skillet heat oil, cook chicken
pieces over medium heat, turning once,
until thoroughly cooked, about 8 minutes.
Drain on paper towels.

Fresh Fruit Skewers

*Choose your favorite fruit for a splash of
color to your platter.*
Servings: 6

Ingredients
6- 8-inch bamboo skewers
12 large fresh blackberries
6- 1-inch cubes cantaloupe
6 fresh strawberries, hulled
6- 1-inch cubes of seedless watermelon
1 kiwi, peeled and cut into 6 pieces

Instructions
Thread each skewer with fruit in the
following order: blackberry, cantaloupe,
strawberry, watermelon, kiwi and end with
another blackberry. Chill until served.

Hot Corn Chip Dip

Servings: 1 1/2cups

Ingredients
4 medium tomatoes, finely chopped
1/2 small onion, finely chopped
1/2 c. celery, finely chopped
1/4 c. green pepper, finely chopped
2 Tbsp. green chilies, chopped
2 Tbsp. red wine vinegar
1/4 c. vegetable oil
1 tsp. mustard seed
salt and pepper to taste
Fritos® Scoop corn chips or raw vegetables

Instructions
Combine tomatoes, onion, celery, green peppers, chilies, vinegar, oil, mustard seed, salt and pepper. Allow mixture to chill 2 hours before serving. If you prefer a hotter dip, add more chopped green chilies. Serve with Fritos® Scoop corn chips or an assortment of raw vegetables.

Mango Salsa

Servings: 2 cups

Ingredients
2 mangoes, seeded, peeled and diced
2 jalapeños, seeded and diced
1/4 c. fresh cilantro, chopped
1/4 c. lime juice
2 tsp. olive oil

Instructions
Combine mango, jalapeños and cilantro; mix well. Add lime juice and olive oil.

Grilled Portabella Mushrooms

Servings: 3

Ingredients
1 Tbsp. olive oil
1 Tbsp. balsamic vinegar
1/2 lb. fresh portabella mushrooms
1/8 tsp. salt
1 dash ground black pepper

Instructions
In a small bowl, mix olive oil and balsamic vinegar. Brush lightly over mushroom surface. Season with salt and pepper. Grill, roast or broil until tender and golden brown.

Appetizers

Chickpea Dip with Toasted Pita Bread

Servings: 4

Ingredients
2 garlic cloves
1- 15.5 oz. can garbanzo beans, rinsed
    and drained
3 Tbsp. lemon juice
3 Tbsp. olive oil, divided
1/2 tsp. salt
2 Father Sam's™ regular white or wheat
    pocket bread

Instructions
1. Preheat oven to 375°F. Place garlic in food processor and pulse until finely minced. Add chickpeas and process until puréed. Add lemon juice, 2 Tbsp. olive oil and salt. Scrape down sides of bowl with rubber spatula. Pulse until smooth (add more lemon juice and olive oil if mixture is too dry). Transfer to a bowl and set aside to let flavors blend.

2. Cut each pita into 8 triangles. Brush with remaining olive oil and bake until lightly golden, about 6 minutes. Serve warm with dip on the side.

Roasted Garlic Bread Rounds

Servings: 16

Ingredients
4 oz. (1/2 c.) garlic cloves
2 c. Kitchen's Best® Chicken stock or
    2 Knorr® Chicken bullion cubes
    dissolved in 2 c. boiling water
aluminum foil
8 slices of French bread

Instructions
1. Preheat oven to 375°F. Cut tops of garlic bulbs and place sliced side down in a shallow baking pan. Add broth and cover pan with aluminum foil. Bake for 1 hour, until cloves in each bulb are soft. Test every 20 minutes by piercing bulbs with a fork. When soft and tender, remove garlic from oven, cool to room temperature. Remove bulbs from broth and discard broth.

2. Remove garlic cloves from bulbs by gently squeezing bottom of each bulb; cloves will pop out. After cloves have been removed, place them in a bowl and mash with a potato masher until a smooth purée. Spread over toasted slices of French bread.

Spinach Turnovers Topped with Sautéed Mushrooms

This is a delicious treat for the spinach lover.
Servings: 16

Ingredients
1 pkg. Giant Eagle® Home-Style
    refrigerated biscuits
1/2 lb. spinach, chopped
1 onion, chopped
1/4 tsp. each salt and pepper
1 Tbsp. lemon juice
1 Tbsp. olive oil
1 Tbsp. Fleischmann's® Unsalted butter
1 garlic clove, minced
1 c. mushrooms

Instructions
1. Preheat oven to 375°F. Roll out biscuits on a floured surface until 1/8-inch thick. Mix together chopped spinach, onion, salt, pepper, lemon juice and olive oil. Place 2 Tbsp. of the filling mixture in center of each rolled out biscuit. Fold to form a triangle and press edges together with a fork. Place on a greased cookie sheet. Bake for 20 minutes.

2. While turnovers are cooking, in a skillet, melt butter. Sauté mushrooms with garlic until mushrooms are soft, about 10 minutes. When ready to serve place mushrooms on top of turnovers.

Italian Style Stuffed Mushrooms

Servings: 16

Ingredients

24 mushrooms, stalks removed
4 Oscar Mayer® Low Sodium bacon strips
2/3 c. white wine
1 lb. Bob Evans® Savory Sage
    sausage, cooked
3 tomatoes, sliced thin
2 green bell peppers, sliced thin

Instructions

1. In a skillet cook sausage until done.

2. Preheat oven to 350°F. Using a spoon, carefully hollow out inside of mushrooms; reserve pulp. Place mushrooms in a lightly greased baking pan, hollowed side up. Slice bacon strips into pieces. Place pieces of bacon inside each mushroom, followed by 1/2 tsp. of wine; set aside remaining wine (about 5 Tbsp.). Chop reserved mushroom pulp very fine and mix with chopped sausage. Press mixture into mushroom caps and press in firmly. Fill above the top by 1/2-inch.

3. Pour remaining wine on top of mushrooms. Bake for 40 minutes. While mushrooms are cooking, slice thin, tomatoes and green peppers. On a serving platter, place sliced tomatoes followed by sliced green peppers. Place cooked mushrooms on top of tomatoes and green peppers. Serve hot.

Marinated Mushroom Caps

Servings: 16

Ingredients

1/3 c. white wine vinegar
1/3 c. vegetable oil
2 green onions, trimmed and chopped
2 Tbsp. chopped fresh parsley
1/2 tsp. each salt, dry mustard and
    crushed dried basil
1/4 tsp. ground black pepper
1 lb. mushrooms, cleaned and
    stems removed

Instructions

1. Combine vinegar, oil, green onions, parsley, salt, dry mustard, basil and pepper; stir well. Set aside.

2. Carefully remove and discard stems. Add caps to vinegar mixture, toss gently and coat evenly. Refrigerate for 4 hours in an airtight container.

Davey's Stuffed Mushrooms

A superb stuffed mushroom recipe.
Servings: 24

Ingredients

1 lb. small/medium mushrooms
1/2 lb. Bob Evans® Savory Sage sausage
4 garlic cloves, minced
1 c. Tops® Cornflake and Toasted Corn
    Cereal, finely crushed
2 hard boiled eggs, chopped
1/2 c. (1 stick) Fleischmann's® Unsalted
    margarine, melted
1/4 tsp. each of garlic powder, black
    pepper, and oregano
olive oil

Instructions

1. Wash and pull stems off, chop stems and set aside. Hollow out mushroom caps. In a skillet brown 1/2 lb. ground pork sausage, when sausage is almost browned add minced garlic cloves to taste and chopped mushroom stems; drain.

2. Place finely crushed cereal, chopped hard boiled eggs, margarine, garlic powder, black pepper and oregano in a large bowl; mix well. Add sausage mixture to bowl.

3. Stuff mushrooms, dip in olive oil and place in a baking dish. Bake in a 350° oven for 15-20 minutes. Serve hot.

Appetizers

Shrimp in Garlic Sauce
Servings: 6

Ingredients
1/2 lb. small shrimp, shelled
salt
8 Tbsp. olive oil
3 large garlic cloves, peeled and
    coarsely chopped
1 dried red chili pepper, stem and
    seeds removed
1/2 tsp. paprika
1 Tbsp. minced parsley

Instructions
1. Preheat oven to 375°F. Take shells off shrimp. Dry shrimp and sprinkle with a little salt on both sides. Place shrimp on a platter and set at room temperature for 10 minutes.

2. Slice chili pepper in half. Place oil, garlic and chili pepper in ceramic dish and heat in oven until garlic is just golden. Add shrimp, toss in oil and return to oven for 5-10 minutes.

Soft Pretzels
Serve as an appetizer or keep on hand for a snack.
Servings: 12-16

Ingredients
3 1/2 c. all-purpose flour, divided
2 Tbsp. sugar
1 tsp. salt
1 pkg. yeast
1 c. water
1 Tbsp. Fleischmann's®
    Unsalted margarine
1 egg yolk, beaten
1 Tbsp. water
coarse salt

Instructions
1. Mix 1 c. flour, sugar, salt and yeast. Heat together, 1 c. water and margarine. Gradually add to dry mixture and beat 2 minutes. Add 1/2 c. flour; beat on high speed for 2 more minutes. Stir in remaining flour. On a floured board, knead 5 minutes. Turn in greased bowl, cover with a towel and let rise until doubled.

2. Divide dough in 12-16 pieces. Roll into ropes and form a pretzel. Place on a greased cookie sheet. Cover and let rise 15 minutes.

3. Mix egg yolk and 1 Tbsp. water. Brush tops of pretzels with yolk mixture and sprinkle with coarse salt. Bake in a 375°F oven for 15 minutes. Cool on rack.

Breakfast

The
Culinary Guide
for **MSPI**

Breakfast

Sweet Rolls and Breads

Coffee Cakes and Muffins

Eggs and Potatoes

Cinnamon Rolls

These rolls are so delicious they just had to be first.
Servings: 12

Note:
1. Where margarine is listed, use Fleischmann's® Unsalted margarine sticks.

2. If you own a bread machine, place all wet ingredients in machine first, followed by dry, adding yeast last. Set bread machine on 2 lb. and dough. Once dough is finished proceed to step 4.

Ingredients

Dough:
1/4 c. warm water
1 c. apple juice or water
1 egg
4 Tbsp. soft margarine
2 tsp. vanilla extract
4 c. Pillsbury® bread flour
1 1/2 tsp. salt
1/3 c. sugar
1 pkg. or 2 1/4 tsp. dry yeast

Filling:
3/4 c. brown sugar
3/4 c. walnuts (optional)
2 tsp. cinnamon
4 Tbsp. soft margarine

Glaze:
1 1/2 c. powdered sugar
2 1/2 Tbsp. water
2 Tbsp. melted margarine
1 drop of maple extract

Instructions

1. In a bowl dissolve yeast in warm water. Let stand 5 minutes until foamy. Add apple juice, egg, soft margarine, vanilla, salt and sugar; beat until mixture is slightly thickened, about 4 minutes.

2. Add 1/2 c. flour at a time, stirring well each time until dough does not stick to the bowl. Knead dough on a lightly floured surface until smooth and elastic, about 6 minutes, adding small amounts of flour if too sticky.

3. Place dough in a lightly oiled bowl turning once to coat. Cover bowl with plastic wrap and top with a clean kitchen towel. Let dough rise in a warm spot until double in size, about 1 hour. Punch dough down, cover bowl as before, and let rise until again almost double, about 30 minutes.

4. Roll out dough on a floured surface to a 12x16-inch rectangle, long end towards you. Spread 2 Tbsp. soft margarine leaving a 1-inch border along edges.

5. Combine all filling ingredients and mix well. Cover butter with filling pressing it down gently. Snugly roll up dough pinching seams together. Cut dough into 12 equal pieces. Place rolls into pan, brush edges with 1 Tbsp. melted margarine so rolls don't stick.

6. Cover pan with plastic wrap and allow rolls to rise for 45 minutes. Bake in a 350°F oven for 30 minutes. Cool rolls in pan for 15 minutes. As rolls are cooling whisk together ingredients for glaze. Once rolls have cooled, drizzle rolls with glaze.

Glazed Apple-Cinnamon Bowknots

A bowknot design adds a twist to the original round sweet roll.
Servings: 24; 2 loaves

Note: If you own a bread machine, place all wet ingredients in machine first, followed by dry, add yeast last. Set machine on dough and proceed to step 4.

Ingredients

5 1/4 c. all-purpose flour
1 pkg. dry yeast
1 1/4 c. apple juice
1/2 c. Fleischmann's® Unsalted margarine
1/3 c. sugar
1/2 tsp. salt
2 eggs
1 tsp. cinnamon
1/4 c. water

Apple Glaze:
1 c. sifted powdered sugar
1 tsp. cinnamon
1 to 2 Tbsp. apple juice (enough to make icing easy to drizzle)

Instructions

1. In a large bowl combine 2 c. of flour and yeast; set aside. In a medium saucepan heat and stir apple juice, margarine, sugar and salt just until warm and margarine almost melts. Add mixture to dry mixture along with eggs. Beat with mixer on low to medium for 30 seconds, scraping bowl. Beat on high for 3 minutes. Using a wooden spoon blend cinnamon, water and remaining 2 c. flour.

2. Turn dough onto floured surface. Knead in remaining flour (enough to make a moderately soft dough that is smooth and elastic). Shape dough into a ball. Place in a lightly greased bowl; turn once. Cover; let rise in a warm place until dough doubles in size, about 1 hour.

3. Punch dough down. Turn onto lightly floured surface. Divide in half. Cover and let rest 10 minutes. Meanwhile, lightly grease 2 baking sheets; set aside.

4. Roll each portion of the dough into a 12 x 7-inch rectangle. Cut each rectangle into twelve 7-inch long strips. Tie each strip loosely in a knot. Arrange knots 2-inches apart on prepared baking sheets. Cover and let rise in a warm place until nearly double in size, about 30 minutes.

5. Bake in a 400°F oven for 12 minutes or until golden. Remove rolls from baking sheets. Cool on wire racks. Combine ingredients for apple glaze; mix well. Drizzle over bowknots.

Sweet Rolls and Breads

Specialty Crepes

These crepes are my dad's specialty.
Servings: (17) 6-inch crepes or
(11) 9-inch crepes

Ingredients
2 large eggs
1 c. apple juice or orange juice
1/3 c. water
1 c. all-purpose flour, preferably bleached
1/4 tsp. salt
2 Tbsp. Fleischmann's® Unsalted
    margarine, melted
2 or 3 tsp. Fleischmann's® Unsalted
    butter for coating pan
jelly, marmalade, fresh fruit or
    anything you desire to place
    inside and atop crepes

Instructions
1. In a large bowl mix eggs, juice, water, flour, salt and margarine until blended. Cover and refrigerate for 2 hours or up to 24 hours.

2. Melt 2 tsp. butter to coat small skillet. Pour 1/2 c. batter in skillet, moving pan from side to side so batter covers pan evenly. Cook until lightly brown lifting edges with spatula. Remove and place in a 200°F oven to keep warm until ready to serve. Repeat. Serve crepes with anything you desire. We prefer fresh fruits and jams.

Apple Pancakes

Servings: 4

Ingredients
1 c. all-purpose flour
1 Tbsp. sugar
2 tsp. baking powder
1/4 tsp. salt
1 beaten egg
1 c. apple juice
2 Tbsp. apple sauce
1 apple, peeled and thinly sliced

Instructions
1. In a medium bowl, stir together flour, sugar, baking powder and salt. Make a well in center of dry mixture, set aside.

2. In another bowl, combine egg, water and apple sauce. Add mixture to dry mixture. Stir just until moistened, batter should be a little lumpy.

3. Heat skillet and lightly grease. Using a soup ladle, pour about 1/4 c. of batter onto hot skillet. Cook over medium heat until pancake begins to bubble, about 2 minutes. Once pancake bubbles flip on other side; cook until golden brown on each side. If pancakes are thin, thicken by adding 1 Tbsp. of flour at a time to batter. Serve warm topped with syrup and fresh sliced apples.

Sweet Rolls and Breads

Baked French Toast with Citrus Sauce

Most recipes for French toast call for milk. I modified this recipe by using orange juice in place of milk. The orange juice adds a sweet citrus taste.
Servings: 4

Ingredients
2 Tbsp. Fleischmann's®
    Unsalted margarine
3 Tbsp. wheat germ
1/2 c. orange juice
2 Tbsp. honey
6 egg whites
12 slices French bread, 1-inch thick

Citrus Sauce:
1/4 c. sugar
1 Tbsp. cornstarch
1 1/4 c. orange juice
2 tsp. Fleischmann's® Unsalted margarine
1 medium banana, sliced

Instructions
1. Heat margarine in a 9x13-inch pan until melted. Sprinkle 3 Tbsp. wheat germ evenly over margarine.

2. Beat orange juice, honey and egg whites until foamy. Dip bread into egg mixture and place in pan. Drizzle remaining egg mixture over bread.

3. Bake in a 450°F oven for 10 minutes. Turn bread over, bake 7 minutes or until bottom is golden brown.

Citrus Sauce:
1. In a small saucepan, combine sugar and cornstarch. Stir in orange juice.
Cook and stir over medium heat until thick and bubbly. Cook and stir 2 minutes.

2. Remove from heat. Stir in margarine until melted then add sliced bananas and pour over French toast.

Sweet Rolls and Breads

Pumpkin Bread

Servings: 1 loaf

Ingredients
1 c. all-purpose flour
1 c. brown sugar, packed
1 Tbsp. baking powder
1 tsp. ground cinnamon
1/4 tsp. of each salt, baking soda
    and nutmeg
1/8 tsp. ground ginger
1 c. Libby's® 100% Pure Pumpkin
1/2 c. water
2 eggs
1/3 c. shortening
1 c. all-purpose flour
1/2 c. chopped walnuts (optional)
1/2 c. raisins (optional)

Instructions
1. Grease bottom and sides of a 9x5x3-inch loaf pan; set aside. In a large mixing bowl combine 1 c. flour, brown sugar, baking powder, cinnamon, salt, baking soda, nutmeg and ginger. Add pumpkin, water, eggs and shortening. Beat with mixer on low speed until blended. Beat on medium to high speed for 2 minutes. Add 1 c. flour; beat until blended. Fold in walnuts and raisins.

2. Spoon batter into prepared pan. Bake in a 350°F oven for 60-65 minutes or until wooden toothpick inserted near center comes out clean. Cool in pan on wire rack for 10 minutes. Remove loaf from pan. Cool completely on wire rack.

Strawberry Bread

Servings: 2 loaves

Ingredients
3 c. all-purpose flour
2 c. sugar
3 tsp. cinnamon
1 tsp. salt
1 tsp. baking powder
1 1/4 c. vegetable oil
4 eggs
2- 10 oz. pkg. sliced frozen
    strawberries, thawed
1 c. nuts, chopped (optional)
powdered sugar

Instructions
1. Combine flour, sugar, cinnamon, salt and baking powder in a large mixing bowl. In a small bowl, combine oil, eggs and strawberries. Make well in center of dry ingredients and pour into two well greased loaf pans.

2. Bake in a 350°F oven for 1 hour or until toothpick inserted in center comes out clean. Remove from pans and cool. Dust with powdered sugar before serving.

Fischl's Cranberry Banana Bread

This is my grandmother's recipe; it's filled with polka dots of tart red cranberries. Did you know February 23rd is National Banana Bread Day?
Servings: 24 slices; 2 loaves

Ingredients

1 c. mashed ripe bananas
1 c. fresh or canned whole cranberries
1 c. sugar
1/2 c. Fleischmann's® Unsalted margarine
1/2 c. water
2 large eggs
2 c. all-purpose flour
1 tsp. baking powder
1 tsp. baking soda

Instructions

1. Preheat oven to 375°F. Using a wood or plastic spoon, mix ingredients in order given. (Do not use a mixer. It beats the batter too smooth, giving bread a cake like texture). Fold in cranberries. Batter should be lumpy.

2. Spoon batter into 2 greased and floured 1 1/2 qt. bread pans. Bake for 35 minutes or until tooth pick inserted in center comes out clean. Remove from oven. Immediately remove loaf from pan and place on wire rack until cool to the touch. Place bread in an airtight container or re-sealable plastic bag and store in refrigerator.

Monkey Bread

Servings: 6

Ingredients

4- 12 oz. cans Giant Eagle® Biscuits Home-Style
1 1/2 tsp. cinnamon
1 c. brown sugar
3/4 c. (1 1/2 sticks) Fleischmann's® Unsalted margarine
1 c. white sugar
nuts and/or raisins (optional)

Instructions

1. Grease a Bunt cake pan. Cut each biscuit into quarters. Mix together cinnamon and brown sugar in a plastic bag. Shake biscuits in bag and drop into pan. Place nuts and or raisins in between layers.

2. In a small saucepan, melt margarine. Add sugar and bring to a boil. Pour butter mixture over biscuits. Bake in a 350°F for 45 minutes. Immediately invert onto a foil covered dish. Serve warm. Pick pieces off and enjoy!

Sweet Rolls and Breads

Stollen
Servings: 3 loaves

Ingredients
4 1/2 c. all-purpose flour
1 pkg. active dry yeast
1/4 tsp. ground cardamom
1 1/4 c. orange juice
1/2 c. Fleischmann's® Unsalted margarine
1/4 c. sugar
1 tsp. salt
1 egg
1 c. raisins or currants
1/4 c. diced mixed candied fruits and peels
1/4 c. blanched almonds (optional)
1 Tbsp. finely shredded orange peel
1 Tbsp. finely shredded lemon peel

Glaze:
1 c. sifted powdered sugar
2 Tbsp. hot water
1/2 tsp. Fleischmann's®
     Unsalted margarine
1 drop vanilla extract

Instructions
1. In a large bowl combine 2 c. of flour, yeast and cardamom. In a saucepan heat and stir orange juice, 1/2 c. margarine, sugar and 1/2 tsp. salt until warm and margarine melts. Add egg to flour mixture. Beat with an electric mixer on low speed for 30 seconds, scraping bowl. Beat on high speed for 3 minutes. Stir in as much remaining flour as you can. Stir in raisins, candied fruits and peels, almonds, and orange and lemon peels.

2. Turn dough onto floured surface. Knead in enough remaining flour to make a moderately soft dough. Shape dough into a ball. Place in a lightly greased bowl; turn once. Cover; let rise in a warm place until double in size, about 1 hour.

3. Punch dough down. Turn onto a lightly floured surface. Divide into thirds. Cover and let rest 10 minutes.

4. Meanwhile, lightly grease two baking sheets; set aside. Roll one portion into a 10x6-inch oval. Without stretching, fold long side over to within 1-inch of opposite side; press edges to lightly seal. Place on baking sheet; repeat with remaining dough. Cover; let rise until nearly double, about 1 hour.

5. Bake in a 375°F oven for 18-20 minutes or until golden. Remove from baking sheets; cool 30 minutes on wire rack. In a small bowl, combine powdered sugar, hot water, margarine and vanilla; mix well and brush glaze over warm bread.

Coffee Cakes and Muffins

Apple Coffee Cake

For holidays, my mom makes this apple coffee cake for breakfast. It's delicious and easy to prepare.
Servings: 12

Ingredients

1 package of Duncan Hines® Moist
    Deluxe® classic yellow cake mix
3 eggs
1- 20 oz. can apple pie filling

Crumb Topping:
1/2 c. brown sugar
2 Tbsp. Fleischmann's®
    Unsalted margarine
2 tsp. cinnamon
1/2 tsp. flour
1/4 c. chopped nuts (optional)

Instructions

In a medium bowl combine cake mix, eggs and apple filling and place in a greased 9x13-inch glass pan. In a small bowl combine all ingredients for crumb topping. Mix well and sprinkle on top of filling. Bake in a 300°F oven for 45 minutes.

California Coffee Cake

Servings: 1- 8" cake

Ingredients

1/2 c. Crisco® shortening
1/2 c. sugar
1/2 tsp. vanilla
1 egg
1 1/2 c. all-purpose flour
1/2 tsp. salt
1 1/2 tsp. baking powder
1/2 c. water

Fig Filling:
1/2 c. California dried figs, chopped
1/4 c. chopped walnuts (optional)
1/2 c. brown sugar
1/4 c. Fleischmann's® Unsalted
    margarine, melted
1 Tbsp. cinnamon

Instructions

1. In a large bowl cream together shortening, sugar and vanilla. Add beaten egg and mix thoroughly. Sift flour, salt and baking soda and add alternately with water. Spread half the batter in a greased 8-inch cake pan. Cover with fig filling (see recipe below) and add remaining batter. Bake in a 350°F oven for 45 minutes.

2. To prepare fig filling rinse figs with hot water then chop fine. Blend with walnuts, brown sugar, margarine and cinnamon.

Coffee Cakes and Muffins

German Streusel Coffee Cake

Servings: 12

Ingredients

1/2 c. water
2 Tbsp. sugar
1/4 c. Fleischmann's® Unsalted margarine
1 tsp. salt
1 pkg. dry yeast
1/4 c. very warm water
1 egg
2 c. all-purpose flour

Topping:
1/2 c. all-purpose flour
1/2 c. sugar
1 tsp. ground cinnamon
1/4 c. Fleischmann's® Unsalted margarine

Instructions

1. Boil water; pour into large mixing bowl; add sugar, margarine and salt. Cool to luke-warm.

2. Dissolve yeast in very warm water; add yeast mixture and egg to above mixture and stir well. Add 2 c. flour gradually, beating well after each addition. Cover and let rise until double in size, about 1 hour. Spread in a greased 9x13-inch pan.

3. In a small bowl combine flour, sugar and cinnamon. With a fork or pastry blender, cut in margarine. Sprinkle over mixture in pan. Let rise until double in size, about 30-45 minutes.

4. Bake in a 375°F oven for 20-25 minutes.

Coffee Cakes and Muffins

Apple Sunflower Strudel
Servings: 8; 1 loaf

Ingredients
1 2/3 c. all-purpose flour
1/4 tsp. salt
1 Tbsp. vinegar
2 Tbsp. sunflower oil
1 egg, slightly beaten
1/4 c. warm water
1/4 c. sugar
1/2 c. packed brown sugar
2 Tbsp. Cream® cornstarch
1 1/2 tsp. ground cinnamon
5 1/2 c. tart apples, chopped
1 1/2 Tbsp. lemon juice
1/2 c. and 2 Tbsp. raw sunflower
    kernels, divided
3 Tbsp. Fleischmann's® Unsalted
    margarine, divided
2 tsp. honey

Instructions
1. In a medium bowl, mix flour and salt. Add vinegar, oil and egg. Knead until dough is smooth. Place in a clean bowl. Cover and set aside for 1 hour.

2. For the sugar mixture mix together sugar, brown sugar, cornstarch and cinnamon; set aside.

3. On a floured pastry cloth, roll dough to a 12x8-inch rectangle. Spread apples over dough; sprinkle lemon juice, sugar mixture and 1/2 c. of sunflower kernels over apples. Dot with 2 Tbsp. margarine. Using a pastry cloth to lift pastry, roll dough jelly roll fashion. Seal edges. Place on a lightly greased cookie sheet. Bake in a 400°F oven for 35 minutes.

4. For topping, mix together honey and margarine; spread on top of strudel. Sprinkle remaining 2 Tbsp. sunflower kernels over top. Bake 10 minutes longer.

Coffee Cakes and Muffins

Cranberry Orange Muffins
Servings: 12

Ingredients
1 1/2 c. all-purpose flour
1 c. sugar
2 tsp. baking soda
1/2 c. (1 stick) Fleischmann's® Unsalted
    margarine, melted and cooled
2 large eggs
3/4 c. orange juice
1 Tbsp. grated orange peel
1 c. dried cranberries

Topping:
1/4 c. sugar
1/2 tsp. ground cinnamon

Instructions
1. In a medium bowl, stir together flour, sugar and baking soda. In a separate bowl, stir together margarine, eggs, orange juice, and grated orange peel. Stir liquid mixture into dry mixture until just combined. Stir in cranberries. For topping: In a small bowl stir together 1/4 c. sugar and cinnamon.

2. Spoon batter into 12 paper-lined muffin tins. Sprinkle topping on top of batter. Bake in a 350°F oven for 20-25 minutes or until lightly brown and a toothpick inserted near the center comes out clean.

Red, White and Blue Muffins
Begin the festivities of Independence Day with these patriotic muffins.
Servings: 12 muffins

Ingredients
2 c. all-purpose flour
4 tsp. baking powder
3/4 c. sugar
1 tsp. salt
2 eggs
1/2 c. Fleischmann's® Unsalted
    margarine, melted
1 c. water
1/2 c. each fresh blueberries and
    fresh red raspberries

Topping:
1/8 tsp. cinnamon
1/2 c. sugar

Instructions
1. Sift dry ingredients into a large bowl. Add blueberries and raspberries to dry mixture. In a small bowl beat eggs, add margarine and water. Quickly stir liquid mixture into dry mixture.

2. Fill paper-lined muffin cups 3/4 full and sprinkle lightly with topping mixture. Bake in a 400°F oven for 20 minutes. Happy 4th!

Spinach Fritters
Servings: 8

Ingredients
1 lb. zucchini, peeled and grated
1 lb. potatoes, peeled and grated
1 onion, peeled and grated
2 lbs. spinach, rinsed, stemmed
    and chopped
2 eggs
1/2 c. all-purpose flour
1 Tbsp. salt
1 tsp. ground cumin
1 tsp. coriander
1 tsp. white pepper
2 c. vegetable oil

Instructions
1. In colander, combine peeled and grated zucchini, potatoes and onion; squeeze out as much liquid as possible. Transfer mixture to a large bowl and add spinach, eggs, flour, salt, cumin, coriander and pepper; mix well.

2. Heat oil in large skillet over medium-high heat. Drop in batter by spoonfuls and fry each until golden; drain on paper towel. Keep warm until all fritters are cooked. Serve hot.

Cast-Iron Skillet
This is sure to please the man in your life.
Servings: 6

Ingredients
2 slices Oscar Mayer® Low Sodium bacon
3 medium red potatoes, thinly sliced
1 medium red or green sweet pepper,
    cut into 1/2-inch strips
1 c. chopped onion
1/4 tsp. salt
1/8 tsp. cayenne pepper
1/8 tsp. ground black pepper
1 lb. All Natural® Wellshire Farms™
    Polska Kielbasa
1- 10 oz. package frozen
    whole-kernel corn

Instructions
1. In a large skillet, cook bacon until crisp. Remove bacon, reserving bacon drippings in skillet. Drain bacon on paper towels. Crumble bacon and set aside.

2. Add potatoes to skillet. Cook and stir over medium heat for 5 minutes. Add sweet peppers and onions. Sprinkle with salt and pepper. Cook and stir mixture 8 minutes more. Add sausage and corn. Cook and stir for 8-10 minutes or until potatoes are tender and browned. Sprinkle with crumbled bacon. Serve hot.

Eggs and Potatoes

Eric's Omelets

My husband makes a great omelet. Thank you for cooking mine just right!
Servings: 1

Ingredients
2 eggs
1/8 tsp. salt
1/8 tsp. pepper
non-stick cooking spray
your choice of filling – tomatoes,
    mushrooms, onions, green peppers

Instructions
1. Combine eggs, water, salt and pepper. Beat with fork until combined. Spray pan with cooking spray and add egg mixture to skillet. Cook on medium.

2. As eggs set, run spatula around edge of skillet. When eggs are set remove from heat. Add 1/2 vegetable(s) across center of omelet and fold in thirds. Top omelet with remaining vegetables.

Egg-Stacy Sandwich

When I worked at Perkins Family Restaurant™ during high school, the cooks would make this specialty sandwich for us.
Servings: 1

Ingredients
2 slices bread, toasted and buttered with
    Fleischmann's® Unsalted or Light Butter
1 slice tomato
2 slices Oscar Mayer® Low Sodium bacon
1 egg

Instructions
Cook egg sunny side up – well done. Cook bacon until crisp. Slice tomato and toast bread. Place bacon, egg and tomato on buttered toast, make a sandwich and cut in half.

Eggs and Potatoes

Country Style Bacon and Eggs with Hash Brown Potatoes

There is nothing like bacon and eggs with hash brown potatoes to start a morning off right.
Servings: 2

Ingredients
6 slices Oscar Mayer® Low Sodium bacon
1 Tbsp. Fleischmann's® Unsalted butter
2 c. Ore-Ida® Hash Browns Southern
   Style Potatoes
4 eggs

Instructions
Melt butter in skillet add hash brown potatoes and cook until potatoes are golden brown. Meanwhile in another skillet cook eggs to your liking. In separate skillet cook bacon until crisp. Flavor eggs and potatoes with salt and pepper.

Steak Bruchetta

Hot pepper sauce give these tortillas some zip!
Servings: 4

Ingredients
2 Tbsp. olive oil
1 Tbsp. lime juice
1/4 c. chopped fresh cilantro
3/4 c. chopped fresh tomatoes
1/2 c. chopped red onion
24 oz. beef top sirloin steak
1 1/2 c. green bell peppers, sliced
1 1/2 c. mushrooms, sliced
1 garlic clove, crushed
5 eggs, beaten
1/4 tsp. hot pepper sauce
4- 10-inch Old El Paso® flour tortillas

Instructions
1. In medium bowl, combine olive oil, lime juice, cilantro, tomatoes, red onion, salt and pepper. Place steak in shallow non-metallic container and cover with marinade. Refrigerate for 1 hour.

2. Grill steak for 4 minutes on one side and 1 minute on other side. Remove from heat, dice into small cubes and set aside. In a lightly oiled skillet, cook and scramble eggs to desired firmness. Season with hot pepper sauce, salt and pepper. Pour marinade into medium sauce pan and bring to a simmer over medium heat. Add green peppers, mushrooms and garlic; simmer for 10 minutes.

3. Warm tortillas on grill. Line tortillas with meat and vegetables; place eggs on top. Wrap and serve.

Eggs and Potatoes

Apple Sausage Patties
Servings: 12 patties

Ingredients
1/3 c. chopped and peeled onion
1 lb. Bob Evans® Savory Sage sausage
1 medium apple, peeled, cored and
    finely shredded
1/2 tsp. crushed sage
1/8 tsp. cayenne pepper

Instructions
1. Stir together all ingredients in a large bowl. Shape into (12) 3-inch patties. Cover and refrigerate at least 30 minutes.

2. Heat 10-inch skillet over medium-high heat. Add patties; reduce heat to medium. Cook 5 minutes; turn over. Continue cooking until patties are no longer pink, about 3-5 minutes.

Hearty Brunch Potatoes
This dish has all you need to spice up any breakfast.
Servings: 8

Ingredients
7 medium potatoes
1/2 c. sweet peppers, chopped
1/2 c. green peppers, chopped
1/2 c. frozen corn
1 small onion, chopped
2 garlic cloves, minced
1/2 lb. All Natural® Wellshire Farms™
    Polska Kielbasa
2 Tbsp. olive oil
1/4 tsp. pepper

Instructions
1. Peel potatoes and cut into 1/2-inch cubes and place in saucepan covered with water. Bring to a boil; reduce heat and cook for 10 minutes.

2. Sauté chopped green and sweet peppers, corn, onion and garlic until tender. Cut sausage into small chunks, add to vegetable mixture. Cook, uncovered for 7 minutes. Drain potatoes and add to vegetable mixture. Add oil and pepper and mix well. Place in a 9x13-inch pan. Bake in a 350°F oven for 35 minutes.

Deviled Eggs

Servings: 6

Ingredients
6 hard-cooked eggs
1/4 c. Kraft® Light Mayo
1 tsp. prepared mustard
1 tsp. vinegar
paprika (optional)

Instructions
1. Place eggs in a single layer in a large saucepan. Add enough cold water to come 1-inch above the eggs. Bring to a boil over high heat. Reduce heat so water is just below simmering. Cover and cook for 15 minutes; drain. Cool and peel eggs.

2. Halve eggs lengthwise and remove yolk. Place yolks in bowl and mash with a fork. Add mayonnaise, mustard and vinegar; mix well. If desired, season with salt and pepper. Stuff egg white halves with yolk mixture. Garnish with paprika.

Country Garden Scrambled Eggs

Servings: 4

Ingredients
8 eggs
1 c. finely chopped fully cooked ham
1/4 c. sweet red pepper, chopped
1/4 c. green pepper, chopped
1/4 c. sliced canned mushrooms
1/4 c. chopped onion
4 Tbsp. Fleischmann's®
    Unsalted margarine
1/4 tsp. garlic salt
1/4 tsp. pepper
pinch of celery seed

Instructions
In a bowl, beat eggs; add ham, pepper, mushrooms and onion. Melt margarine in a large skillet; add the egg mixture. Cook and stir gently over medium heat until eggs are completely set. Add garlic, salt, pepper and celery seed.

Eggs and Potatoes

Sunrise Special

Servings: 1

Ingredients

2 Tbsp. olive oil
1 tsp. fresh thyme
1 tsp. fresh rosemary
ground black pepper to taste
1 portobello mushroom, stem removed
    and cap wiped clean on both sides
sea salt
1 large ripe tomato
2 tsp. olive oil
1 egg, lightly beaten
2 tsp. snipped fresh chives

Instructions

1. Mix olive oil with herbs and pepper, brush liberally on both sides of mushroom.

2. Heat skillet over high heat. When hot sprinkle lightly with salt. Add the mushroom to pan and cook, turning several times until golden and cooked through, about 8 minutes. Remove mushroom from pan and keep on a warm plate gill side up, covered loosely with aluminum foil. Leave drippings in pan.

3. Using the same pan, warm a teaspoon of olive oil over medium-high heat. When hot, add tomato slice and sear well on one side only. Sprinkle top (raw) side with a little salt and pepper. Remove tomato, place on mushroom and re-cover. Leave drippings in pan.

4. Melt 2 tsp. olive oil in pan. When hot, add beaten egg and let cook until it starts to set on the bottom. Reduce heat to low and stir, incorporating any bits of mushroom and tomato left in pan. Add chives, salt and pepper and cook until done to your liking. Spoon scrambled egg over tomato and garnish with more snipped chives. Serve hot.

Short Orders

Soups

Salads

Sandwiches

Soups

Italian Sausage Soup with Tortellini

This soup embodies all the wonders of Italian cooking: Italian sausage, garlic, tomatoes and red wine. Serve with hot bread and a salad for a delicious meal.
Servings: 8

Ingredients
1 lb. Johnsonville® Sweet Italian sausage
1 c. onion, chopped
2 cloves garlic, minced
5 c. Swanson's® 99% or 100% fat free
    Beef Broth, or dissolve 5 Herbox® Beef
    bullion cubes in 5 c. of water
1/2 c. water
1/2 c. red wine
4 large tomatoes, peeled, seeded
    and chopped
1 c. thinly sliced carrots
1/2 Tbsp. fresh basil leaves
1/2 tsp. dried oregano
1- 8 oz. can tomato sauce
1 1/2 c. sliced zucchini
3 Tbsp. chopped fresh parsley
8 oz. fresh tortellini pasta

Instructions
1. In a large skillet brown sausage. Remove sausage and drain, reserving 1 Tbsp. of the drippings. Sauté onions and garlic in drippings. Stir in prepared beef broth, water, wine, tomatoes, carrots, basil, oregano, tomato sauce and sausage. Bring to a boil. Reduce heat; simmer uncovered for 30 minutes.

2. Skim fat from soup. Stir in zucchini and parsley. Simmer covered for 30 minutes. Add tortellini during last 10 minutes.

Tomato-Curry Stew

Servings: 2

Ingredients
1/2 c. dry lentils
1 c. water
5 oz. stewed tomatoes
1/8 c. chopped onion
2 stalks celery, chopped, with leaves
1/4 tsp. curry powder
3 cloves garlic, minced
salt and pepper to taste

Instructions
Combine lentils and water; bring to a boil. Lower heat, add tomatoes, onion, celery, curry, garlic and salt and pepper. Cover and let simmer 45 minutes. Check every 15 minutes to stir and add water if necessary.

Soup à la Provence

My uncle and his wife live in Provence. The flavors of Provence, France will be brought to your stovetop with this enticing soup.
Servings: 6

Ingredients
1/2 c. onion, peeled and chopped
1 tsp. garlic, crushed
3 c. Swanson's® 100% fat free Chicken broth, or dissolve 3 Herbox® Chicken bullion cubes in 3 c. boiling water
2 tsp. paprika
1/2 tsp. dried thyme, crushed
1/2 tsp. fennel seed
1/4 tsp. orange peel, grated
1 1/2 lb. tomatoes, cored and diced
1 1/2 lb. potatoes, peeled and diced

Instructions
1. Coat saucepan with cooking spray. Add onion and garlic. Sauté until onion is translucent, about 5 minutes. If using bullion cubes, in separate sauce pan, bring 3 c. water to a boil add 3 bullion cubes to water, stir until dissolved.

2. Add broth, paprika, thyme, fennel seed and orange peel; bring to a boil. Add potatoes and half the tomatoes. Return to boil, reduce heat and simmer, covered, until vegetables are tender, about 10 minutes. Allow to cool slightly. Transfer to a blender in batches and process until smooth.

3. Return to saucepan and bring to a boil. Stir in remaining tomatoes, cover and simmer, until tomatoes are soft, about 5 minutes. Serve hot with a baguette.

Soups

Easy Bean Soup

Servings: 6

Ingredients
1 medium onion, chopped
2 medium carrots, chopped
2 celery stalks, chopped
2 c. water
2- 15 oz. cans navy beans
28 oz. can diced tomatoes, un-drained
1 lb. Bob Evans® Savory Sage
    Sausage, cooked
1 tsp. salt
1/2 tsp. garlic salt
1/2 tsp. paprika
1/2 tsp. dried marjoram
1/2 tsp. dried thyme
1/2 tsp. pepper

Instructions
In a 3-quart saucepan, combine onion, carrots, celery and water. Bring to a boil; boil for 5 minutes. Add remaining ingredients; mix well. Heat through.

Potato Soup

Servings: 6

Ingredients
5 potatoes, diced
1/2 c. onion, chopped
2 stalks celery, chopped
1 tsp. celery salt
2/3 tsp. pepper
8 slices Oscar Mayer® Low Sodium
    bacon, cooked
6 Tbsp. bacon drippings
2 Tbsp. flour
2 c. water

Instructions
1. Dice potatoes and place in boiling water (enough water to just cover potatoes). Cook potatoes for 10 minutes; drain. Meanwhile fry bacon until cooked reserving bacon drippings; crumble cooked bacon.

2. In a large kettle, place potatoes, onions, celery, salt, pepper, bacon, bacon drippings, flour and water. Cook on medium heat adding flour as needed until sauce is slightly thickened. Serve hot.

Beef Vegetable Soup
Servings: 8

Ingredients
1 lb. hamburger
1 1/4 c. onions, chopped
2 c. carrots, chopped
1- 16 oz. can of green beans
1- 16 oz. can of corn
3 celery stalks, chopped
1- 46 oz. V-8® Juice
2 tsp. sugar
1 tsp. celery seed
1/8 tsp. pepper
1 barley leaf

Instructions
Brown hamburger with diced onions; drain. Combine all ingredients and bring to a boil. Cover, reduce heat and simmer for 1 hour. Remove barley leaf before serving. Serve hot.

Soups

French Style Tomato Soup
Servings: 6

Ingredients
6 slices French bread, 1-inch thick
2 Tbsp. extra-virgin olive oil
1 large yellow onion, finely chopped
3 garlic cloves, minced
3 lbs. ripe tomatoes, peeled and seeded,
    then diced
4 c. Kitchen's Best® chicken or
    vegetable stock
1/2 c. basil leaves, finely chopped
6 whole basil leaves
salt and ground black pepper to taste

Instructions
1. Preheat oven to 300°F. Place bread slices on a baking sheet and bake until lightly browned, turning once, 10-15 minutes. Set aside.

2. In a large pot over medium heat, warm oil. Add onions and sauté, stirring frequently, until softened, 5-7 minutes. Add garlic and cook until softened, but not browned, about 30 seconds.

3. Add tomatoes and stock; raise heat to high and bring to a boil. Reduce heat to medium-low, cover and cook until tomatoes are softened, about 30 minutes. Remove from heat.

4. Purée soup with a hand held mixer until desired consistency (you may place soup in blender or food processor. The hand held mixer works just as well and most importantly, one less item to clean up). Add chopped basil and season to taste with salt and pepper.

5. To serve, place a slice of toasted bread in bottom of each warmed bowl. Ladle soup on top and garnish with a basil leaf. Serve hot.

Easy Chicken Noodle Soup

*A delicious and easy recipe for chicken
noodle soup.*
Servings: 4

Ingredients

3 c. water
2 Knorr® Chicken flavored bullion cubes
1 Tbsp. flour (for thicker broth add
    more flour)
1 c. Mrs. Weiss'® Kluski Enriched
    egg noodles
1 c. chopped chicken
1 Tbsp. olive oil
1/2 c. each of mushrooms, green peppers,
    carrots, and onions, diced
1/4 tsp. garlic
1/4 tsp. basil
1/8 tsp. pepper

Instructions

1. Boil water in a large pot. Add bullion cubes to water. Add a little flour at a time to obtain desired thickness (this replaces the gravy). Once cubes have dissolved add noodles.

2. In skillet cook chicken until done. Chop chicken into small bite size pieces and add to pot. In skillet heat olive oil and sauté mushrooms, green peppers, carrots and onions until vegetables are soft. Sprinkle with garlic, pepper and basil. Add vegetables to pot and simmer for 20 minutes on low heat.

Soups

Mediterranean Summer Soup

I found this in my grandma Fischl's recipe file, a recipe from the sunny coast of France.
Servings: 6

Ingredients
1 c. medium onion, chopped
3 Tbsp. olive oil
1 1/2 lbs. tomatoes, peeled, seeded
   and chopped
2 garlic cloves, minced
5 c. Kitchen Best® Chicken Stock
5 c. water
1/4 c. Kraft® Minute® white rice
6 parsley sprigs
1 Tbsp. sugar
salt and pepper to taste
1 bay leaf
1/2 tsp. thyme
4 fennel seeds
garnish with minced parsley

Instructions
In a large skillet, lightly sauté onions in olive oil. Add tomatoes and garlic. Simmer on medium heat for 5 minutes. Transfer to a large soup pot. Add next 7 ingredients. Combine bay leaf, thyme and fennel seeds. Add to soup. Simmer for 30 minutes. Garnish with parsley when ready to serve.

Christmas Eve Chili

Chili has always been a favorite in our home. On Christmas Eve we serve it up in a sourdough bread bowl. We like our chili spicy hot – make to your liking.
Servings: 5

Ingredients
1 lb. ground beef
1- 14 oz. can diced tomatoes
1- 14 oz. can tomato sauce
1- 14 oz. can tomato paste
1 medium onion, diced
1 green pepper, chopped
2- 16 oz can Bush's® Best Chili Beans
1- 1.25 oz. pkg. McCormick®
   Chili Seasoning

Instruction
In a large skillet, cook meat and onions until meat is browned; drain. In a large pot combine cooked meat, onions and remaining ingredients. Bring to a boil. Cover, reduce heat to low and simmer for 20 minutes.

White Chili

The cumin adds a nice southwest bite to this favorite chili.
Servings: 5

Ingredients

3 Tbsp. olive oil
2 lb. chicken breasts
2 Tbsp. chili powder
2 tsp. cumin
2 tsp. oregano
1/4 tsp. crushed red pepper
2 tsp. salt
1/4 c. flour
Ortega® Garden Style Salsa

Instructions

1. Heat oil in a skillet and cook chicken and spices until chicken is done.

Add to skillet:
1/2 c. shredded carrots
1/2 c. medium onion, chopped
1/2 c. celery, chopped
2 tsp. garlic, minced

2. Cook until vegetables are soft. Transfer all to a large pot.

Add to pot:
1- 14 oz. can Swanson's® 100% fat free Chicken broth
1- 15 oz. can Campbell's® Pork and Beans
1- 15 oz. can tomato sauce

3. Let cook over medium heat for 30 minutes. Garnish with salsa.

Salads

Vinegar and Oil Dressing

This is a good basic dressing and may be used whenever a light taste is desired.
Servings: 1/4 cup

Ingredients
1 Tbsp. vegetable or salad oil
1 1/2 Tbsp. vinegar
1/2 tsp. salt
1 1/2 Tbsp. sugar
1/2 tsp. celery seed

Instructions
In a bowl or jar with a tight fitting lid, combine oil, vinegar, salt, sugar and celery seed; mix well.

French Mustard Dressing

Servings: 1 cup

Ingredients
2/3 c. olive oil
1/3 c. vinegar
1 1/2 tsp. tarragon
1 1/2 Tbsp. sugar
1 tsp. salt
1/2 tsp. dry mustard
1/2 tsp. minced garlic

Instructions
In a bowl or jar with a tight fitting lid, combine olive oil, vinegar, tarragon, sugar, salt, dry mustard and garlic; mix well. Store in refrigerator.

Marinated Fruit Salad

Servings: 6 cups

Ingredients
3 c. cantaloupe
1- 13.5 oz. can pineapple chunks, drained
1- 10.5 oz. can mandarin oranges, drained
1 c. strawberries, hulled
1- 6 oz. can frozen lemonade
1/4 c. orange marmalade
2 Tbsp. orange liquor (optional)

Instructions
Combine fruits in a bowl. Combine lemonade, marmalade and orange liquor. Pour over fruits; stir gently. Chill at least 2 hours before serving.

Strawberry and Roasted Chicken Salad with Strawberry Vinaigrette Dressing
Servings: 8

Ingredients
1- 16 oz. bag of red leaf lettuce
1/2 lb. strawberries
1/4 c. walnuts or pecans (optional)
2 c. roasted chicken
salt and pepper to taste

Dressing:
1 oz. red wine vinegar
3 oz. strawberry jam (homemade jam preferred)
2 oz. olive oil

Instructions
Wash and dry lettuce. Place lettuce in a large salad bowl. Cut strawberries in half. If using walnuts or pecans, chop and add to salad. Slice roasted chicken into bite size pieces. Add salt and pepper to taste.

Dressing:
Mix together vinegar, strawberry jam and olive oil; shake until well blended.

Pita Salad
Servings: 6

Ingredients
2 Schwebel's™ Old World Flat Bread, white, Italian herb or wheat
8 romaine lettuce leaves, torn into bite-size pieces
2 green onions, chopped
1 cucumber, chopped
3 tomatoes, cut into wedges

Dressing:
1/4 c. chopped fresh parsley
1 clove garlic, peeled and chopped
2 Tbsp. lime juice
1/4 c. lemon juice
1/4 c. olive oil
1/4 tsp. each salt and ground black pepper
1/4 c. chopped fresh mint leaves

Instructions
Preheat oven to 350°F. Toast pitas 5-10 minutes in preheated oven, until crisp. Remove from heat, and break into bite size pieces. In a large salad bowl, toss together toasted pita pieces, romaine lettuce, green onions, cucumbers and tomatoes.

Dressing:
In a small bowl, mix parsley, garlic, lime juice, lemon juice, olive oil, salt, pepper and mint. Pour over pita mixture; toss together just before serving.

Dill Chicken Salad

*Serve with Giant Eagle® Biscuits Home-Style
and fresh lemonade for a perfect lunch.*
Servings: 4

Ingredients
1 lb. skinless, boneless chicken breasts
1 c. dry white wine
1 sprig fresh dill weed
1/8 tsp. freshly ground black pepper
1 1/2 c. seedless grapes
1 c. thinly sliced celery
8 red leaf lettuce leaves, washed
1/2 c. chopped salted cashews (optional)
5 sprigs fresh dill weed, for garnish

Dressing:
1/2 c. Kraft® Mayo
1/4 c. green onions, minced
2 Tbsp. fresh dill, chopped
1/4 tsp. freshly ground black pepper

Instructions
1. Arrange chicken in medium skillet and add wine, dill and pepper. Season with salt. Simmer over medium low heat until chicken is just cooked through, turning once (about 11 minutes). Transfer chicken to plate and let cool.

2. Cut chicken into 1/2-inch pieces. Place in a large bowl. Add grapes and celery and mix in dressing to thoroughly coat mixture. Season with salt and pepper to taste. Cover and refrigerate for at least 20 minutes to develop the flavors. Arrange lettuce leaves on each plate, mound on salad and sprinkle with nuts. Garnish with fresh dill.

Dressing:
Whisk mayonnaise, green onions, dill and pepper in a small bowl to blend (can be made one day ahead). Cover and chill.

Charleston Crab Salad

*I modified this salad after eating a
similar salad at a restaurant in Charleston,
South Carolina.*
Servings: 4

Ingredients
3 c. fresh spinach, rinsed, dried and torn
   into bite-size pieces
2 c. leaf lettuce, rinsed, dried and torn
   into bite-size pieces
1 c. finely shredded cabbage
2- 10.5 oz. can mandarin orange segments
1 red onion, sliced in rings
2- 6 oz. cans Chicken of the
   Sea® Crabmeat

Dressing:
1/2 tsp. orange zest
3 Tbsp. orange juice
2 Tbsp. balsamic vinegar
2 tsp. olive oil
1 tsp. fresh chopped tarragon

Instructions
In a large bowl, combine spinach, lettuce, cabbage, oranges and onions. Add crabmeat and gently toss until combined. Set aside.

Dressing:
In a small jar with a tight-fitting lid, combine orange zest, orange juice, vinegar, oil and tarragon. Cover and shake until well mixed. Pour orange dressing over spinach salad and gently toss until salad is well coated.

Macaroni Garden Salad

A pasta salad with lots of veggies.
Servings: 5

Ingredients
1- 16 oz. pkg. macaroni
2 cucumbers, peeled and diced
4 tomatoes, chopped
1 onion, finely diced
4 stalks celery, diced
1- 15 oz. can peas, drained
1 c. Kraft® Miracle Whip dressing
1 head iceberg lettuce

Instructions
In a large pot of lightly salted boiling water, cook macaroni until al dente, about 10 minutes. Rinse cooked macaroni under cold water and drain. In a large bowl, combine macaroni, cucumbers, tomatoes, onion, celery, peas and dressing; mix well. Chill for 1 hour then serve on crisp lettuce leaves.

Salads

French Café Summer Salad

A fresh and colorful salad full of flavor and loved every time I serve it. Serve cold on a hot summer day with a loaf of crusty French bread
Servings: 8

Ingredients
14 medium red potatoes
2 c. shredded red cabbage
1- 1oz. can whole kernel corn, drained
1 large red onion, diced
1 red bell pepper, diced
1 green bell pepper, diced
1 yellow bell pepper, diced
1 cucumber, diced
salt and ground black pepper to taste

Dressing:
1/4 c. olive oil
2 garlic cloves, crushed
2 Tbsp. Grey Poupon® Dijon Mustard
    made with white wine

Instructions
1. Place potatoes in a large pot with lightly salted water to cover. Bring to a boil over medium-high heat, and cook until tender, but still firm about 20 minutes. Drain, cool and cut into bite-size pieces.

2. In a large salad bowl add cabbage, corn, onion, peppers and cucumbers. Mix in cooled potatoes.

Dressing:
In a small bowl, whisk together olive oil, garlic and Dijon mustard. Mix dressing in salad until salad is well coated. Season with salt and pepper. Chill for 1 hour before serving.

Spinach-Rotini Salad

Servings: 4

Ingredients
1 c. rotini pasta
1- 10 oz. bag baby spinach
1 c. mushrooms, sliced

Dressing:
1/2 c. red wine vinegar
1/2 c. vegetable oil
1/2 tsp. salt
1/4 tsp. ground black pepper

Instructions
Cook pasta according to package directions, rinse with cold water and drain to cool. In a large salad bowl, combine pasta, spinach and mushrooms.

Dressing:
In a small bowl combine vinegar, oil, salt and pepper; mix well. Pour dressing over salad.

Sandwiches

Aunt Dorothy's Sloppy Joes
Servings: 6

Ingredients
6 Schwebels® Kaiser rolls
1 lb. ground beef
1 large onion, diced
1- 8 oz. can tomato soup
1 c. ketchup
1/2 c. brown sugar
1 Tbsp. vinegar
salt and pepper to taste

Instructions
Brown meat with diced onions. Once meat is cooked through transfer to a large pot. Combine soup, ketchup, brown sugar, vinegar, salt and pepper to taste and add to pot with meat and onions. Simmer for 30 minutes.

America's Classic Hamburger
Servings: 6

Ingredients
1 lb. ground beef
dash salt and pepper
6 Schwebels® Kaiser rolls
garnish with tomato, onion, lettuce,
    pickle, ketchup and mustard

Instructions
Heat grill. Place beef in a medium bowl, add salt and pepper to taste. Mix and prepare beef patties. Place patties on grill and cook to your liking. Serve hamburgers in rolls and add garnish. Serve with seasoned potato wedges found on page 61.

Sandwiches

Savory Beef Slow Cooked Sandwiches

This sandwich is terrific for lunch or dinner. The spices are just enough to give the tender roast a full flavor.
Servings: 8

Ingredients
8 French bread style rolls, lightly toasted
1 boneless chuck roast halved (3 - 4 lbs.)
1 Tbsp. dried minced onion
1 tsp. of both garlic powder and
    dried oregano
1 tsp. of each dried rosemary, caraway
    seeds, dried marjoram, celery seed
1/4 tsp. cayenne pepper
1 medium onion, sliced

Instructions
Combine all ingredients in a small bowl and mix well. Rub mixture over roast. Place seasoned roast in a slow cooker and cook on low for 5 hours. Before serving lightly shred meat with a fork, it should easily pull apart. Serve on lightly toasted French style rolls.

Note: Slow cookers may vary in cooking length.

Slow Cooked Beef Barbecue

Servings: 12

Ingredients
12 French bread style rolls, lightly toasted
4 lbs. cubed stew meat
2- 8oz. cans tomato sauce
1 medium onion, chopped
1/2 c. vinegar
1/4 c. firmly packed brown sugar
2 tsp. salt

Instructions
Place beef in slow cooker. Combine remaining ingredients. Pour over beef. Cook on low for 5 hours. Before serving lightly shred meat with a fork, it should easily pull apart. Serve on lightly toasted French style rolls.

Turkey and Corned Beef
Rueben Sandwich
Servings: 1

Ingredients
2 slices Millbrook® Cleveland Rye bread, lightly toasted
1 Tbsp. sauerkraut
2 slices corned beef
2 slices turkey breast
1 Tbsp. Kraft® Light Done Right® Creamy French Style dressing
1 Tbsp. Kraft® Mayo
Lettuce
1 Tbsp. Fleischmann's® Unsalted butter

Instructions
Marinate sauerkraut in dressing for 1/2-hour. Butter slices of bread; spread sauerkraut on top. Cover with corned beef and turkey. Place lettuce on top of meats and top with mayonnaise.

Turkey and Veggy Pitas
This recipe is from Eric's aunt, Mary Wise. Mary is a fabulous cook and this sandwich is just one of her many outstanding dishes.
Servings: 4

Ingredients
1 lb. ground turkey
1/2 c. green peppers, chopped
1/2 c. medium onion, chopped
1- 20 oz. package frozen California Blend
1/2 c. water
1/4 tsp. ground ginger
4 tsp. Cream® corn starch
1/4 c. Kraft® Mayo
1/4 c. water chestnuts
4 Father Sam's™ regular white or wheat pocket bread

Instructions
1. Brown turkey in a large skillet add peppers and onions. Sauté until onions are transparent. Add California Blend, heat until cooked through.

2. In a separate bowl combine water, ginger, corn starch and mayonnaise. Stir until cornstarch is dissolved. Add to skillet along with water chestnuts and heat through until thickened.

3. Cut pita pockets in half and toast on light setting in toaster. Stuff skillet mixture into pitas and serve.

Sandwiches

Curried Chicken Salad Sandwiches
Servings: 4

Ingredients
1/2 c. dry white wine
pinch of salt
10 black peppercorns
3 Tbsp. fresh lemon juice (1 lemon)
2 sprigs fresh thyme
4 boneless, skinless chicken breasts
1 Tbsp. canola oil
1/2 onion, finely chopped
1 Tbsp. curry powder
1/2 c. Kraft® Mayo
1 c. red or green grapes, halved
1/4 c. sliced almonds, toasted (optional)
freshly ground black pepper
8 slices Roman Meal® 100% Whole
    Grain bread
4 lettuce leaves

Instructions
1. In a large saucepan combine wine, salt, peppercorns, lemon juice and thyme. Add chicken breasts and enough water to cover. Bring liquid to a boil, reduce heat and simmer for 10 minutes. Remove from heat and let chicken cool in the liquid.

2. In a small saucepan, heat oil over medium-low heat. Add onions and cook until onions are soft, about 5 minutes. Add curry powder and cook for 2 more minutes. Remove from heat and cool. Stir in mayonnaise.

3. When chicken is cool enough to handle, remove from liquid; discard liquid. Cut chicken into small pieces, place in bowl and toss with curried dressing, grapes and almonds. Season to taste with salt and pepper. Refrigerate until ready to serve. Serve on bread or stuff inside a pita pocket.

Sun-Dried Tomato Basil BLT

I love a crisp BLT. I added a little twist by using flat bread. The sun-dried tomato basil adds zip to an already great sandwich.
Servings: 1

Ingredients

1 slice of Delections® Sun-dried Tomato Basil Flat-out Bread
2 Tbsp. diced tomatoes
2 leaves of lettuce
2 strips Oscar Mayer® Low Sodium bacon or Louis Rich® Turkey bacon
2 Tbsp. Kraft® Miracle Whip dressing or Kraft® Mayo

Instructions

In skillet cook bacon until crisp. Spread dressing across entire surface of flat bread. Chop tomato, lettuce, and bacon and place in center of flat bread. Wrap tightly and cut in half. This sandwich is great with a bowl of French Style Tomato Soup (recipe found on page 39).

Tomato and Tuna Salad Burst

This burst of tomato and tuna is a pretty display.
Servings: 1

Ingredients

1 large tomato, hollowed
1 can tuna, drained well
2 celery stalks
3 egg whites
3 Tbsp. Kraft® Mayo real mayonnaise
1 1/2 Tbsp. fresh lemon juice (1/2 lemon)

Instructions

Hollow out a tomato. Lightly salt and pepper inside tomato. Boil eggs. Remove yolk. Dice egg whites and celery stalks. Mix lightly tuna, celery, egg whites, mayonnaise and lemon juice. Place enough tuna mixture inside tomato that the tuna mixture goes over top of tomato about 1/2-inch.

Sandwiches

Maryland Crab Cakes

Servings: 8

Ingredients

4 slices French bread
1 lb. fresh crabmeat
1/4 c. Kraft® Mayo
1/2 tsp. dry mustard
1/4 tsp. salt
1/8 tsp. ground pepper
1 Tbsp. fresh lemon juice
2 Tbsp. Fleischmann's®
    Unsalted margarine
4 lemon wedges for garnish

Instructions

1. In a blender, pulse 2 bread slices to make crumbs; place on a large plate. Cut remaining bread into 1/4-inch cubes.

2. In a bowl, mix crab, mayonnaise, mustard, salt, pepper, lemon juice and bread cubes just until combined. Cover and refrigerate for 1 hour.

3. In a nonstick skillet, melt margarine over medium heat. Meanwhile, scoop crab mixture by scant 1/2 c. and shape each into 3-inch patties; coat each patty lightly with crumbs. Add crab cakes to skillet. Cook 9 minutes or until golden on both sides and heated through, turning over once. Garnish with a lemon wedge.

Cajun Grilled Fish Sandwich with Pepper-Onion Relish
Servings: 4

Ingredients
4- 4 oz. fresh or frozen skinless white
    fleshed fish fillets, 1/2 - 3/4-inch thick
1 Tbsp. lemon juice
1 tsp. Cajun seasoning
4 Brownberry® white sandwich buns,
    split and toasted

Pepper-Onion Relish:
1 large onion, quartered
1 large sweet pepper, quartered
1 Tbsp. olive oil
3 Tbsp. fresh parsley, snipped
1 1/2 Tbsp. sugar
2 Tbsp. cider vinegar
2 Tbsp. balsamic vinegar
1/4 tsp. salt
1/4 tsp. ground black pepper

Instructions
1. Thaw fish, if frozen. Rinse fish; pat dry with paper towels. Brush fish with lemon juice. Sprinkle Cajun seasoning evenly over all sides.

2. Place fish on grill. Grill until fish flakes easily with a fork, 4-6 minutes. Remove fish from grill. Serve fillets on buns and top with pepper-onion relish; recipe as follows.

Pepper-Onion Relish:
1. Brush onion and sweet pepper with olive oil. Grill onion and sweet pepper uncovered on medium heat for 8-10 minutes, until vegetables are tender, turning occasionally as they cook. Don't char vegetables.

2. Transfer grilled vegetables to cutting board and let cool. Chop vegetables and place in a small bowl. Stir in parsley, sugar, vinegars, salt and pepper. Toss mixture to coat well.

Salmon Sandwich

Servings: 6

Ingredients

1/4 c. Fleischmann's® Unsalted margarine
1/2 c. onion, chopped
2 eggs, beaten
1/4 c. parsley, chopped
1 tsp. dry mustard
1/2 tsp. salt
16 oz. canned salmon, crab or tuna
1/2 c. Nabisco® Original Premium Saltine
    Crackers, crushed
1 c. oil
6 French style rolls
Kraft® Light Mayo

Instructions

1. In a small pan cook onion in margarine until tender. In a large bowl combine onion, eggs, parsley, dry mustard, salt and salmon together; mix well. Divide mixture into six equal parts and shape each part into a round patty. Place crushed cracker crumbs on a small plate; flip each patty twice in the crumbs.

2. In a pan heat oil on medium-high heat. Carefully place patties into the pan. Cook patties until bottom sides are brown then turn over and brown the other side. Place cooked patties in toasted rolls and top with mayonnaise.

Grand Accompaniments

The
Culinary Guide
for MSPI

Grand Accompaniments

Fruit and Vegetable Side Dishes

Breads

Fruit and Vegetable Side Dishes

Cranberry Apple Casserole

This cranberry apple casserole tastes more like a dessert.
Servings: 8

Ingredients
1- 21 oz. can apple pie filling
1- 16 oz. can whole berry cranberry sauce
1/4 c. Fleischmann's® Unsalted margarine
1 1/2 c. rolled oats
3/4 c. brown sugar

Instructions
1. Preheat oven to 350°F. Combine apple pie filling and cranberry sauce in a shallow baking dish.

2. In a medium bowl, mix margarine, oats and brown sugar until crumbly. Sprinkle mixture evenly over fruit. Bake in oven for 40 minutes, or until browned and crisp.

Yam and Apple Casserole

Servings: 6

Ingredients
1 lb. yams, peeled and sliced
2 large apples, cored and sliced
2/3 c. apple juice
2 Tbsp. cornstarch
3 Tbsp. water
1/3 c. sugar
1/2 tsp. ground cinnamon
1/3 c. wheat germ

Instructions
1. Preheat oven to 375°F. Grease a 2-quart casserole dish. Alternately layer yams and apples in dish; set aside.

2. In a saucepan, heat apple juice. Mix cornstarch with water in a small bowl. When juice boils, stir in cornstarch mixture; cook, stirring until thickened. Stir in sugar and cinnamon. Spoon sauce over yams and apples. Sprinkle wheat germ on top. Bake until apples are tender, 25-30 minutes.

Fruit and Vegetable Side Dishes

Colorado Pineapple Casserole

Servings: 6

Ingredients
1 c. Fleischmann's® Unsalted margarine
1 c. sugar
4 eggs
1- 20 oz. can crushed pineapple,
    undrained
1 loaf French bread ripped into
    small pieces with crust on

Instructions
In a large bowl cream margarine and sugar. Add eggs one at a time. Add undrained pineapple. Fold into bread. Place in a 2-quart casserole dish. Bake in a 350°F oven for 30-45 minutes or until golden brown on top.

Royal Brown Rice with Mushrooms

Servings: 6

Ingredients
1 Tbsp. vegetable oil
2 c. sliced mushrooms
1/2 c. green onion, chopped
3 c. Kraft® Minute® brown rice

Instructions
Cook rice according to package directions. Meanwhile, in a saucepan, heat oil over medium heat. Add mushrooms and green onions, cook until tender. Add cooked brown rice; toss lightly and heat thoroughly before serving.

Fruit and Vegetable Side Dishes

Baked Vegetable Medley

An easy recipe when there is not much time to cook.
Servings: 4

Ingredients
3 c. cauliflowerets
1 c. mushrooms, chopped
1/2 c. cooked Oscar Mayer® Low
    Sodium bacon, chopped
1 Tbsp. olive oil
2 tsp. lemon juice
2 tsp. cider vinegar
1/2 tsp. salt
1/4 tsp. pepper
2 garlic cloves, minced
1/3 c. green onions, chopped

Instructions
Preheat oven 350°F. Grease a 9-inch baking pan. Mix all ingredients except green onions. Place mixture in dish and bake uncovered for 45 minutes, stirring occasionally. Sprinkle with green onions.

Roasted Sweet Potatoes

Servings: 6

Ingredients
3 sweet potatoes, peeled and sliced
    1/3 -inch thick
1 Tbsp. olive oil
salt to taste

Instructions
1. Preheat oven to 450°F. Spread sweet potato slices out on a baking sheet.

2. Brush potatoes with olive oil and sprinkle with salt. Roast potato slices on top oven rack until tender, about 15 minutes.

Fruit and Vegetable Side Dishes

Rosemary Potatoes

Servings: 8

Ingredients

5 large potatoes, cut into 1/8
1/4 tsp. salt
2 green onions, diced
1 tsp. crushed dried rosemary leaves
2 Tbsp. olive oil

Instructions

1. Grease 8x8-inch pan. In a 6-quart pot, boil water adding 1/4 tsp. salt. Place cut potatoes in water and boil for 10 minutes; drain.

2. Sprinkle potatoes with green onions and rosemary. Drizzle with oil; stir to coat. Bake uncovered in a 350°F oven for 20 minutes, stirring occasionally until potato skins are crisp and potatoes are tender.

Parsley Potatoes

These potatoes are so delicious; flecked with a simple mixture of parsley and garlic, there is no need for butter.
Servings: 4

Ingredients

1 lb. red potatoes, diced
1 Tbsp. olive oil
1/4 c. fresh parsley, chopped
1 garlic clove, peeled and minced
1/2 tsp. salt
1/4 tsp. ground black pepper

Instructions

Boil potatoes in salted water until tender, about 10 minutes; drain well. In a small bowl combine oil, parsley, garlic, salt and pepper; mix well. Toss potatoes to coat. Serve hot.

Fruit and Vegetable Side Dishes

Seasoned Potato Wedges

Servings: 4

Ingredients
1/4 c. Fleischmann's® Unsalted margarine
1/4 c. ketchup
1 tsp. Dijon style mustard
1/2 tsp. paprika
1/4 tsp. salt
3 large potatoes or 9 small red
    potatoes, unpeeled
1/4 c. Ruffles® Original potato chips, finely
    crushed or Tops® Cornflake and
    Toasted Corn Cereal, finely crushed
1 Tbsp. Good Season® Italian seasoning

Instructions
1. In a pan over low heat melt margarine, remove from heat and stir in ketchup, mustard, paprika and salt. Cut each potato into 4 wedges. Place potato skin side down on a lightly greased cookie sheet. Brush with 1/3 margarine mixture.

2. Bake in a 425°F oven for 35 minutes or until fork tender; brushing potatoes every 15 minutes with remaining margarine mixture. Sprinkle potatoes with crushed potato chips or cereal and seasoning during last 5 minutes of baking.

Creamy Mashed Potatoes

These mashed potatoes are one of the best comfort foods.
Servings: 6

Ingredients
2- 14 oz. cans Swanson's® 100% fat free
    Chicken broth – see note below
5 large potatoes cut into 1- inch pieces
1/2 c. water
2 Tbsp. Fleischmann's® Unsalted
    margarine or butter
generous dash of ground pepper

Instructions
1. Place broth and potatoes in saucepan. Heat to a boil. Cover and cook over medium heat, 10 minutes or until potatoes are tender; drain, reserving broth.

2. Mash potatoes with 1/4 c. broth, water, butter and pepper. Add additional broth if needed until desired consistency.

Note: Swanson's® 99% fat free Chicken broth contains soy protein.

Fruit and Vegetable Side Dishes

French Potato Salad
An elegant version of the classic potato salad.
Servings: 6

Ingredients
2 lbs. baby red potatoes, scrubbed
1/2 small red onion, peeled and
    thinly sliced

Dressing:
1/3 c. olive oil
1/4 c. red wine vinegar
2 Tbsp. capers (optional)
2 Tbsp. chopped fresh oregano
1 1/2 Tbsp. brown mustard
1/2 tsp. salt
1/4 tsp. ground black pepper
1/8 tsp. hot pepper sauce

Instructions
1. Cook potatoes in boiling water until tender, about 12 minutes; drain and set aside. While potatoes cook, whisk together oil, vinegar, capers, oregano, mustard, salt, pepper and hot pepper sauce; set aside.

2. In a large bowl, combine potatoes and sliced onions; pour dressing over top and toss gently to combine. Serve chilled or at room temperature.

Grilled Corn on the Cob
Serve hot off the grill for a guaranteed summertime favorite
Servings: 4

Ingredients
4 ears of corn, keep husks on
6 c. water
1/2 tsp. salt
4 Tbsp. Fleischmann's®
    Unsalted margarine
dash of salt and white pepper

Instructions
1. Fill kitchen sink or large pot with water and salt. Place corn, with husks on, in water and let soak for 1 hour.

2. Heat grill. Take corn from water and place on grill. Turn corn every so often. Grill corn until husks char a little, about 10 minutes.

3. Remove husks. On each cob, place 1 Tbsp. of margarine and dash of salt and pepper. Serve hot.

Fruit and Vegetable Side Dishes

Zucchini and Tomato Galette

Colorful vegetables wrapped in a pie crust.
Servings: 6

Ingredients
2 yellow squash sliced lengthwise
2 zucchini sliced lengthwise
1 1/2 tsp. olive oil
1/4 tsp. salt
1 Pillsbury® refrigerated piecrust
1/2 c. Nabisco® Original Premium saltine
    crackers, finely crushed
2 Tbsp. chopped basil
4 tomatoes, sliced
1 egg white, beaten

Instructions
1. In a mixing bowl toss squash and zucchini with oil and salt. Cook on grill 10 minutes turning once.

2. Place pie crust on a baking sheet. In a small bowl, combine finely crushed crackers and basil and spread in middle of pie crust.

3. Arrange half of grilled slices in spoke fashion to cover mixture. Place tomato slices over squash; arrange remaining squash slices over tomatoes. Fold outer edge of dough over vegetables. Brush top of crust with egg white.

4. Bake in a 400°F oven for 30 minutes. Serve warm.

Honey Glazed Carrots

Servings: 2

Ingredients
5 medium carrots, peeled
1/3 c. water
1/4 tsp. salt
2 Tbsp. honey
2 tsp. lemon juice
1/4 tsp. ground cinnamon

Instructions
Cut carrots into 1/2-inch coin shapes. Place carrots, water and salt in a small saucepan; cook until tender; drain. Place carrots back in saucepan and add honey, lemon juice and cinnamon. Cook over medium heat, stirring gently until carrots are glazed, about 5 minutes.

Fruit and Vegetable Side Dishes

Oven-Roasted Veggies
Servings: 8

Ingredients
3 medium potatoes, peeled and cut into 1-inch pieces
2 medium carrots, halved lengthwise and cut into 2-inch pieces
1 medium onion cut into wedges
1 green pepper, cut into chunks
1/4 c. olive oil
1 tsp. dried basil
1 Tbsp. lemon juice
3 garlic cloves minced
1 tsp. salt
1/2 tsp. pepper
1 red sweet pepper cut into strips
1 tomato, cut into wedges

Instructions
1. In a greased 9x13-inch pan combine potatoes, carrots, onion and green pepper. Combine oil, herb, lemon juice, garlic, salt and pepper. Drizzle over vegetables; toss to coat.

2. Bake covered in a 325°F oven for 45 minutes, stirring once. Increase oven to 450°F. Add sweet pepper strips and tomatoes, toss and bake uncovered for 20 minutes stirring occasionally.

Marinated Cucumber Salad
Servings: 8

Ingredients
4 c. cucumbers, unpeeled and sliced
1/2 medium red onion, sliced
1 green pepper, diced
2 large celery stalks, sliced
1/2 c. white vinegar
1/4 c. salad oil
3/4 c. sugar
1 Tbsp. salt
1- 4 oz. jar Dromedary® pimentos

Instructions
Toss cucumbers, onion, green pepper and celery in a large bowl. In a small saucepan combine vinegar, oil, sugar and salt and bring to a boil. Boil for 1 minute stirring constantly. Pour over vegetable mixture. Add pimentos. Chill over night in refrigerator. Toss when ready to serve.

Fruit and Vegetable Side Dishes

Homemade Baked Beans

Regardless, someone brings this dish to a family gathering. It's a must have!
Servings: 5

Ingredients
1- 16.5 oz. can Bush's® Best Original baked beans
1- 8 oz. can tomato sauce
1- 8 oz. can tomato paste
1/2 lb. Oscar Mayer® Low Sodium bacon, diced
1 lb. brown sugar
1 tsp. mustard

Instructions
Combine all ingredients. Cook in slow cooker on low for 5 hours.

Calico Beans

My mother-in-law, Mary, gave me this recipe. I gave Pieter a serving for dinner one evening and had to follow up with 3 more servings.
Servings: 6

Ingredients
1/2 lb. ground hamburger
1/2 lb. Oscar Mayer® Low Sodium bacon, diced
1 onion, chopped
1/2 c. ketchup
2 Tbsp. vinegar
1/2 c. brown sugar
1- 15 oz. can kidney beans, drained
1- 15 oz. can Campbell's® Pork and Beans
1- 15 oz. can lima beans, drained

Instructions
1. In a skillet cook hamburger, diced bacon and chopped onion until browned; drain off grease.

2. In a bowl combine hamburger mixture, ketchup, vinegar, brown sugar and beans until blended. Place in a 9x13-inch baking dish. Bake uncovered in a 350°F oven for 55 minutes. Serve hot.

Fruit and Vegetable Side Dishes

Spicy Beans

Servings: 6

Ingredients
1/2 c. Kraft® Minute® brown
    rice, uncooked
2- 15 oz. cans red beans
2 jalapeño peppers, seeded and chopped
1 tsp. ground cumin
1 Tbsp. chili powder
2 green onions, chopped
black pepper to taste

Instructions
1. Preheat oven to 350°F. Cook rice according to package directions. Meanwhile, pour beans into a 2-quart casserole dish. Sprinkle with jalapeños, cumin, chili powder and black pepper.

2. Bake in oven for 30 minutes. Sprinkle with green onions. Serve beans over cooked rice.

---

7 Layer Salad

Servings: 8

Ingredients
1 head lettuce, broken into bite size pieces
1 1/2 c. chopped celery
4 hard boiled eggs, sliced
1- 10 oz. package frozen peas
1/2 c. green pepper, diced
1 sweet onion, sliced thin
Hormel® Real Bacon pieces
2 c. Kraft® Miracle Whip dressing
2 Tbsp. sugar

Instructions
1. In a large salad bowl place in this order: lettuce, celery, eggs, peas, green peppers and onions. Sprinkle over top layer with bacon pieces.

2. In a small bowl mix together dressing and sugar. Pour dressing on top of bacon pieces. Cover tightly and let set overnight. Toss together before serving.

Fruit and Vegetable Side Dishes

Summer Vegetables in Angel Hair Pasta

Servings: 8

Ingredients

1- 16 oz. package angel hair pasta
2 c. onions, peeled and chopped
2 c. tomatoes, chopped
1 1/2 c. green beans, trimmed
1 c. yellow squash, washed and trimmed
1 c. zucchini, washed and sliced
2/3 c. water
2 Tbsp. chopped fresh parsley
1 garlic clove, crushed
1/2 tsp. chili powder
1/4 tsp. salt
1/8 tsp. ground black pepper
1- 6 oz. can tomato paste

Instructions

1. In a large pot cook pasta according to package directions; drain. While pasta cooks, combine onions, tomatoes, green beans, squash, zucchini, water, parsley, garlic, chili powder, salt and pepper; cook for 10 minutes on medium-low heat.

2. Stir in tomato paste; cover and cook on low for 15 minutes, stirring occasionally, or until vegetables are tender. Spoon sauce over warm pasta. Serve hot.

Fruit and Vegetable Side Dishes

Stir-Fried Noodles and Vegetables

Servings: 4

Ingredients

2 tsp. vegetable oil
1 garlic clove, minced
1 dried red chili pepper
1/2 c. carrots, cut diagonally
1 red bell pepper, cut into thin strips
1/4 lb. fresh pea pods
1/2 c. Mrs. Weiss'® Enriched Medium
    Egg Noodles, cooked

Instructions

1. In large pot cook noodles according to package directions; drain.

2. Heat Wok or large skillet over medium-high heat. Add oil, garlic, dried red pepper, carrots and red bell pepper strips; stir-fry 3 minutes. Add pea pods; continue to stir-fry 2 minutes. Add cooked noodles; cook and stir until hot. Discard dried red pepper.

Breads

Note: For the first 3 bread recipes (Garlic Herb Focaccia, Braided Bread and Rosemary Onion Bread) you may use a bread machine. Refer to your bread machine regarding the sequence of ingredients. For example, my bread machine requires placing wet ingredients first, followed by dry, ending with yeast.

Garlic Herb Focaccia

Focaccia is flat Italian bread. This bread is delicious by itself, as pizza crust or served with a plate of warm pasta.
Servings: 2 loaves

Note: If using a bread machine, place first 4 ingredients in machine. Settings are: 1 lb. and dough. Once dough is completed start with instruction number 3.

Ingredients
1 c. warm water, divided
2 1/2 c. all-purpose flour
1/2 tsp. salt
1/2 pkg. active dry yeast

1 Tbsp. olive oil
6 garlic cloves, peeled and minced
1 tsp. fresh rosemary, chopped
1 tsp. fresh Italian parsley, chopped
1/4 tsp. coarse salt

Instructions
1. In a large bowl, dissolve yeast in 1/4 c. warm water. Let stand 5 minutes until foamy. Add remaining water, flour and salt. Beat until dough forms.

2. Turn dough out on a lightly floured surface and knead until elastic, about 10 minutes. Place in an oiled bowl, cover and let rise in a warm place for 1 hour or until double in size. Punch dough down and knead a few times. Return to oiled bowl, cover and let rise again until double in size; about 1 hour.

3. Preheat oven to 400°F. Lightly grease two baking sheets.

4. After dough has risen the second time, press air out and divide in half. On a floured surface, roll each half into a 9x12-inch rectangle. Place on prepared baking sheets and brush breads with olive oil. Scatter garlic, oregano, rosemary and parsley over surface of each and press lightly. Sprinkle with salt. Bake about 20 minutes or until golden. Serve warm.

Braided Bread

My daughter Megan, enjoys kneading and braiding the dough; a rewarding way to break bread together as a family.
Servings: 2 loaves

Note: If using a bread machine place ingredients in order given, except for the 1 Tbsp. of water and egg yolk. Settings are 2 lb. and dough. Once dough is completed start with instruction number 5.

Ingredients
1/2 c. and 2/3 c. warm water
5 large eggs
1 c. vegetable oil
7 c. all-purpose flour
3/4 c. and 1 Tbsp. sugar
2 tsp. salt
2 tsp. active dry yeast

1 large egg yolk
1 Tbsp. water

Instructions
1. In a small bowl combine 1/2 c. warm water, yeast and 1 Tbsp. sugar; stir to dissolve yeast. Let set in warm spot until foamy, about 10 minutes.

2. Using an electric mixer beat 5 eggs until foamy. Add dissolved yeast, oil, salt, and remaining 3/4 c. sugar; beat until mixture is pale yellow and slightly thickened, about 4 minutes. Add 2/3 c. warm water and beat to blend.

3. Add 1/2 c. flour at a time, stirring well each time until dough no longer sticks to the bowl. Knead dough on a lightly floured surface until smooth and elastic, about 6 minutes, adding a Tbsp. of flour at a time if dough is too sticky.

4. Place dough in a lightly oiled bowl turning it once to coat. Cover bowl with plastic wrap and top with a clean kitchen towel. Let dough rise in a warm spot until double in size, about 1 hour. Punch down dough, cover bowl as before, and let dough rise 30 minutes more.

5. Grease 2 baking sheets. Turn dough onto a lightly floured surface and divide it in half. Divide each half into 3 equal pieces and roll into 9-inch ropes. For each loaf, braid together 3 ropes, working on a prepared baking sheet. Cover each loaf with a towel and let dough rise until almost double, about 30 minutes. Meanwhile, preheat oven to 400°F.

6. Whisk together egg yolk and 1 Tbsp. water and lightly brush mixture on top of loaves. Bake bread for 10 minutes in a 400°F oven, then lower oven temperature to 350°F and bake for 25-30 minutes or until loaves are golden brown and sound hollow when tapped.

Breads

Rosemary Onion Bread

Servings: 1 loaf

Note: If using a bread machine, place first 7 ingredients in machine. Settings are: 1 lb. and dough. Once dough is completed start with instruction number 3.

Ingredients
1 c. warm water
1 c. whole-wheat flour
1 1/2 c. all-purpose flour
1 Tbsp. fresh rosemary, chopped
1 tsp. salt
1/2 tsp. sugar
1 packet active dry yeast
1 Tbsp. olive oil
1 medium onion, peeled and chopped

Instructions
1. In a large mixing bowl, sprinkle yeast over warm water; let stand for 5 minutes or until mixture becomes foamy.

2. Heat oil in a small skillet over medium-high heat. Add onions and sauté until softened and edges start to turn golden brown, 5 minutes.

3. Stir rosemary, salt and sugar into yeast mixture. Add onions and whole wheat flour and mix. Add enough all-purpose flour to form a soft dough. Turn out onto floured surface and knead 5 minutes. Place in a clean, oiled bowl and cover with a clean kitchen towel. Let rise in a warm place for 1 hour, or until double in size.

4. Preheat oven to 400°F. Punch dough down. Roll up and place in a 9x5x3-inch loaf pan. Bake for 35-40 minutes or until a hollow sound is heard when tapped.

Bruschetta
Servings: 6

Ingredients
1 loaf baguette bread, sliced thin
1/4 c. olive oil
1 garlic clove, minced
4 tomatoes, chopped
balsamic vinegar
8 fresh basil leaves, torn
1 small red onion

Instructions
1. Preheat oven to 375°F. Arrange bread slices on an ungreased cookie sheet. Combine oil and garlic; brush onto bread. Bake 5-8 minutes or until lightly toasted.

2. Combine tomatoes with basil. Sprinkle lightly with vinegar and ground pepper. Remove bread from oven, top with tomato mixture then with sliced red onion. Serve hot.

French Bread
Servings: 2 loaves

Ingredients
2 1/4 tsp. yeast
1/2 tsp. and 1/2 Tbsp. sugar
1 1/2 c. warm water, divided
1 Tbsp. oil
1/2 Tbsp. salt
4 1/2 c. unbleached all-purpose flour
1 egg white
sesame seeds

Instructions
1. Dissolve yeast and 1/2 tsp. sugar in 1/4 c. warm water, set aside. Put 1 1/4 c. warm water in a large mixing bowl; add yeast mixture, oil and salt. Add 2 c. flour and mix to batter state. Add 1/2 Tbsp. sugar. Gradually add 2 1/2 c. more flour. When dough can't be mixed with spoon, roll out and place dough in mixing bowl. Cover and let rise until double in size; about 1 1/2 hours.

2. Remove from bowl and cut into two parts. Form into French loaves and place breads on ungreased baking sheet. Slash loaves diagonally, baste top with egg white and sprinkle with sesame seeds. Cover and let rise 30 minutes or until double in size.

3. Bake in a 350°F oven for 30 minutes or until golden brown. Cool breads on a wire rack.

Breads

Easy Dinner Rolls
Servings: 2 dozen rolls

Ingredients
1 c. warm water
2 pkg. active dry yeast
1/2 c. (1 stick) Fleischmann's®
 Unsalted margarine
1/2 c. sugar
3 eggs
1 tsp. salt
4 c. unbleached all-purpose flour
2 Tbsp. Fleischmann's® Unsalted butter

Instructions
1. Combine warm water and yeast in a large bowl. Let mixture stand until yeast is foamy, about 5 minutes. Stir in margarine, sugar, eggs and salt. Beat in flour, 1 c. at a time, until dough is too stiff to mix. Cover and refrigerate for 2 hours.

2. Grease a 13x9-inch baking pan. Turn chilled dough out onto a lightly floured board. Divide dough into 24 equal-size pieces. Roll each piece into a round ball; place balls in even rows in prepared pan. Cover and let dough balls rise until double in size; about 1 hour.

3. Preheat oven to 375°F. Bake until rolls are golden brown, 15-20 minutes. Brush warm rolls with melted butter. Break rolls apart before serving.

Onion Bread

This bread requires advanced planning and preparation. It's worth the wait!
Servings: 2 loaves

Ingredients

Sponge:
1/2 c. warm water
1/2 tsp. active dry yeast
1 c. bread flour

Carmelized Onions:
2 Tbsp. olive oil
2 large onions, peeled and sliced into
 1/4-inch rings
2 Tbsp. brown sugar

Dough:
1 c. warm water
1 tsp. active dry yeast
2 1/4 c. bread flour
1/2 c. whole-wheat flour
2 1/4 tsp. salt
1/2 tsp. ground black pepper

Instructions

Preparing Sponge:
Place warm water in a small bowl. Sprinkle yeast over water and let sit 3-4 minutes, until foamy. Mix in bread flour. Cover with plastic wrap and let sit overnight in a cool, dry spot.

Carmelizing Onions:
Onions may be prepared the day before. Heat oil in a large skillet over medium heat. Add onions and cook, stirring frequently, for 10 minutes, or until softened and golden brown. Sprinkle with brown sugar and cook another 5-10 minutes, stirring often. Onions should be dark brown, soft and sweet. Remove from heat and cool. Refrigerate until ready to make bread.

Preparing Dough:
1. Place warm water in a large mixing bowl. Sprinkle with yeast and let sit until foamy, about 3-4 minutes. Add prepared sponge, bread flour, whole-wheat flour, salt and pepper. With an electric mixer, mix dough for 2 minutes. Let dough rest for 15 minutes.

2. Add caramelized onions and resume mixing until dough is silky and elastic and pulls away from sides of bowl. The dough should be very wet and sticky, but still elastic. Transfer dough to a lightly oiled bowl and cover with a clean kitchen towel or plastic wrap. Let rise in a warm place for 1 1/2 hours, or until double in size.

3. Turn a baking sheet upside down and sprinkle with flour and cornmeal; set aside. Turn dough onto a well floured surface, handling it gently to preserve as much volume as possible; cut into 2 equal pieces. Gently pull and stretch each piece of dough into a flat round, about 1 1/4-inches thick. Transfer to prepared baking sheet. Cover and let rise in warm place for 45 minutes to 1 hour.

4. Preheat oven to 450°F, place baking stone on middle oven rack to preheat. Before placing loaves in oven, using a spray bottle, quickly sprits oven walls with water. Immediately slide loaves off of baking sheet and onto hot stone. Bake for 16-18 minutes, or until breads are golden brown. Transfer breads to a wire rack to cool.

Breads

Scones
Servings: 14 scones

Ingredients
2 c. all-purpose flour
2 Tbsp. sugar
1 Tbsp. baking powder
1/2 tsp. salt
6 Tbsp. Fleischmann's® Unsalted margarine
1 egg, beaten
1/2 c. water
1 egg, slightly beaten

Instructions
1. In a bowl stir together flour, sugar, baking powder and salt. Cut in margarine until mixture resembles coarse crumbs. Add beaten egg and water, stirring just until dough sticks together. Knead dough gently on lightly floured surface. Cut dough in half.

2. Shape each half into a ball and roll to a 6-inch circle about 1/2-inch thick. With a knife cut each circle into 7 wedges. Place wedges on an un-greased baking sheet. Brush scones with slightly beaten egg. Bake in a 425°F oven for 12-15 minutes.

The Main Event

The
Culinary Guide
for MSPI

The Main Event

Specialty Meats

Chicken and Turkey

Seafood

Pasta

The Main Event

Specialty Meats

Roast Leg of Lamb with Rosemary

This leg of lamb is marinated overnight. Be prepared for many requests for seconds.
Servings: 7

Ingredients
1/4 c. honey
2 Tbsp. Grey Poupon® Dijon-style mustard
2 Tbsp. chopped fresh rosemary
1 tsp. freshly ground black pepper
1 tsp. lemon zest
3 cloves garlic, minced
5 lb. whole leg of lamb
1 tsp. coarse sea salt

Instructions
1. In a small bowl, combine honey, mustard, rosemary, ground black pepper, lemon zest and garlic. Mix well and apply to lamb. Cover and marinate in refrigerator overnight.

2. Preheat oven to 450°F. Place lamb on rack in roasting pan and sprinkle with salt to taste. Bake in a 450°F oven for 20 minutes. Reduce heat to 400°F and roast for 55-60 more minutes for medium rare.

Black Pepper Pork Chops

My mother-in-law, Mary, gave me this delicious recipe for pork chops.
Servings: 4

Ingredients
3 Tbsp. fresh lemon juice
3 green onions, thinly sliced
3 garlic cloves, minced
1 1/2 tsp. diced rosemary
1/2 tsp. black pepper
4 pork chops

Instructions
Preheat oven to 400°F. In a bowl combine lemon juice, scallions, garlic, rosemary and black pepper. Place pork chops in a greased 8-inch pan, lightly spray pork chops with cooking spray and pour mixture over pork chops. Bake for 15-20 minutes.

Specialty Meats

Slow Cooked Apricot Glazed Pork Roast
Servings: 7

Ingredients
2 Herbox® Beef bullion cubes to 2 c. boiling water
1- 18 oz. jar apricot preserves
1 large onion, chopped
2 Tbsp. Dijon-style mustard
4 lb. boneless pork loin roast

Instructions
1. Boil water. Place bullion cubes in water until cubes dissolve. Mix broth, preserves, onion and mustard in a slow cooker. Add pork roast and turn to coat. Cover and cook on low for 5 hours or until done.

2. For a thicker sauce, (remove pork roast from slow cooker) mix 2 Tbsp. cornstarch and 2 Tbsp. water. Stir into slow cooker. Cover and cook on high 10 minutes or until mixture boils and thickens.

Orange Beef Stir-Fry
Servings: 4

Ingredients
1 tsp. Cream® cornstarch
1 c. orange juice
1 lb. trimmed beef, thinly sliced
1 Tbsp. oil
1/4 tsp. crushed red pepper flakes
1 garlic clove, minced
1 Tbsp. grated fresh gingerroot
1/4 c. green onion, thinly sliced
1/4 c. bell pepper, thinly sliced
2 c. Kraft® Minute® white rice

Instructions
1. In a small bowl, combine cornstarch and orange juice. Set aside.

2. In wok, add beef, oil, and red pepper flakes. Stir-fry over high heat until beef is browned. Remove beef with slotted spoon. Set aside. Meanwhile, cook rice according to package directions.

3. Add garlic, gingerroot, onion and bell pepper to oil remaining in wok. Stir-fry for 2 minutes. Add cornstarch/orange juice mixture. Simmer until thickened. Add beef and toss with sauce. Serve over prepared rice.

Specialty Meats

Beef and Mushroom Fajitas

These zesty fajitas are quick and easy to prepare. A sure crowd pleaser.
Servings: 4

Ingredients
1 Tbsp. olive oil
1 lb. lean beef, cut into thin strips
2 tsp. chili powder
1 tsp. dried oregano, crushed
1/8 tsp. each salt and ground black pepper
1 onion, cut into thin strips
1/2 lb. white mushrooms, thinly sliced
2 green onions, chopped
1/2 lime, juiced
3/4 c. Oretga® Salsa - Thick and Chunky
1 avocado, peeled, seeded, sliced
8 Old El Paso® flour tortillas

Instructions
Heat oil over medium-high heat in a large skillet. Add beef strips; brown on all sides, about 3 minutes. Add chili powder, oregano, salt and pepper to taste. Add onion and mushrooms and cook until soft, about 4 more minutes. Add green onion and lime juice. Mix well. Serve with salsa, avocado slices and warm tortillas.

Beef à la Bourguignonne

Servings: 8

Ingredients
1 Tbsp. vegetable oil
2 lb. round steak, cubed
2 onions, peeled and sliced
1/2 lb. mushrooms, trimmed and sliced
1 1/2 Tbsp. all-purpose flour
1/2 tsp. salt
1/4 tsp. ground black pepper
1 c. red wine
1/2 c. Swanson's® 99% or 100% fat free beef broth

Instructions
1. Add oil to heated skillet and sauté round steak, stirring constantly, until browned, about 10 minutes. Remove beef and set aside.

2. Add onion and mushrooms to the same skillet; sauté until onions are translucent, 5-7 minutes. Remove and set aside. Return beef to skillet; sprinkle with flour, salt and pepper. Stir in red wine and beef broth, bring to a boil. Cover, reduce heat, and let simmer for 1 1/4 hours, or until tender. Add sautéed mushrooms and onions before serving.

Specialty Meats

Steak au Poivre

Servings: 2

Ingredients
1 tsp. peppercorns
1 lb. round steak
2 Tbsp. brandy
1 Knorr® Beef bouillon cube, crushed

Instructions
1. Coarsely crack peppercorns and sprinkle both sides of round steak; pressing in firmly. Place steak in refrigerator for 30 minutes.

2. Grill or broil steak to your liking. Meanwhile in a small saucepan, stir brandy and bouillon cube until boiling. Pour over steak before serving.

Italian Pot Roast

Servings: 6

Ingredients
1- 2 1/2 lb. boneless beef round roast
1 medium onion
1/4 tsp. salt
1/4 tsp. pepper
2- 8 oz. cans tomato sauce
1- 0.7 oz. package Good Season® Italian
    dressing mix

Instructions
Place roast in slow cooker and chunk onion on top of roast. Add remaining ingredients. Cover and cook on low for 5 hours.

Wisconsin Brats-n-Beer

My grandmother would make this recipe for brats when we went to visit her in Manitowoc, Wisconsin. She only used Johnsonville® brats.
Servings: 6

Ingredients
6 Johnsonville® Beer 'n Bratwurst®
1 can of beer
2 large onions
6 Schwebel's™ Sweet Harvest Wheat
    hot dog buns

Instructions
Place brats in a 9x13-inch pan. Cover with sliced onions and 1-inch of beer. Cover pan with aluminum foil and cook in a 300°F oven for 3 1/2 hours, turning brats once. Serve brats in toasted buns.

Veal Roast Provençal

Servings: 12

Ingredients

4 Tbsp. dried parsley
2 tsp. olive oil
1 1/4 tsp. thyme
1/4 tsp. each of garlic powder, salt
    and pepper
3 lb. veal
1- 14 1/2 oz. can whole tomatoes
1/3 c. white wine
1- 16 oz. box noodles

Instructions

1. Do not preheat oven. Combine parsley, olive oil, thyme, garlic, salt and pepper. Rub over veal. Place roast, fat side up, on rack in shallow roasting pan. Insert a meat thermometer; do not add water or cover. Roast at 325°F until thermometer registers 155°F, approximately 1 1/4 hours.

2. Transfer veal to a warm platter; let stand for 15-20 minutes. Drain whole tomatoes, reserving the liquid. Chop tomatoes. Drain the fat from roasting pan then add tomatoes, reserved liquid and wine; stirring well. Bring to a boil. Reduce heat to medium-high and cook until slightly thickened, about 3 minutes.

3. Meanwhile, prepare noodles according to package directions; drain. Serve veal roast on top of noodles.

Specialty Meats

Spicy Italian Sausage with Sautéed Vegetables

This dish was made the night before we left for vacation. I scrambled what ever we had left in the refrigerator. This dish has become a family favorite.
Servings: 4

Ingredients
1 Tbsp. olive oil
4 Johnsonville® mild Italian sausage (for spicier flavor choose Hot style sausage)
1/2 orange sweet pepper, sliced
1/2 green pepper, sliced
1/2 medium onion, sliced
Spaghetti enough for 4 persons
1 Tbsp. basil

Instructions
1. Cook spaghetti according to package directions. Meanwhile, boil sausage for 7 minutes to remove the fat. Heat oil in a large skillet. Transfer sausage to skillet, cook until lightly browned. Add peppers and onions, sauté until sausage is browned and vegetables are tender.

2. When spaghetti is done, drain and add basil; mixing basil lightly into spaghetti. Serve sausage mixture on top of spaghetti.

Glazed Country Ham

This is for you Pieter!
Servings: 10

Ingredients
5 lb. ham
1 c. brown sugar
1/4 c. pineapple juice
1 tsp. dry mustard

Instructions
1. Place ham in covered roaster. Add cold water, enough to cover ham. Soak for 12 hours.

2. After soaking, remove ham from water and discard water. Lightly scrub ham. Return ham to pot, add water to cover, and bring to a boil over high heat. Reduce heat, cover and simmer for 2 1/2 hours. Add water to keep it covered. When ham is done, remove ham from liquid and place on a rack, fat side up. Cool for 20 minutes. Remove skin and all but 1/4-inch of the fat. Score ham in a diamond pattern.

3. Combine sugar, juice and mustard and apply by brushing over entire surface. Bake in a 375°F oven for 30 minutes, basting several times with glaze. Allow to cool before carving.

Mom's Meatloaf

One of my mom's specialties.
Servings: 6 slices

Ingredients

1 egg
3/4 c. Tops® Cornflake and Toasted Corn
   Cereal, finely crushed
2 Tbsp. Good Season® Herb and Garlic
   dried seasoning
1/4 c. V-8® juice
1/4 c. onion, diced
1 lb. ground beef

1/2 c. ketchup
1/4 c. brown sugar

Instructions

1. In a medium mixing bowl beat egg. Place cereal and seasoning in plastic bag and crush until very fine. Add to egg seasoned cereal, juice and onions. Add ground beef and mix well.

2. Place mixture in a loaf pan and pat down. Bake in a 350°F oven for 50 minutes, or until no pink remains.

3. Mix ketchup and brown sugar. Put ketchup mixture on top of meat loaf during last 20 minutes in oven.

Dad's Beer Can Chicken

A whole chicken is placed on top of a beer can. It may sound silly, but it is absolutely delicious.
Servings: 8

Ingredients
1 whole chicken
1 can of beer
1/4 tsp. onion salt
1/4 tsp. pepper
1/4 tsp. seasoning salt
1/4 tsp. hickory flavor

Instructions
1. Combine all ingredients and rub over entire chicken. Make a tray out of aluminum foil. Open beer and pour 1/3 of beer into tray. Place tray on grill.

2. Set chicken over beer can and place on tray. Grill on low fire for 1 hour, checking every 15 minutes to ensure there is liquid in the tray at all times; add beer or water as needed. Remove chicken from can and cut as desired. Enjoy the succulent flavor!

Grilled Chicken Breasts with Apple-Cranberry Glaze

Servings: 4

Ingredients
2 Tbsp. red wine vinegar
2 Tbsp. sugar
1/2 c. apple preserves or jam
2 Tbsp. finely diced dried cranberries
salt and pepper to taste
4- 5 oz. boneless, skinless chicken breasts
1 Tbsp. olive oil

Instructions
1. In a small saucepan, heat vinegar and sugar over medium heat until mixture boils and sugar dissolves. Add apple preserves or jam, whisk in dried cranberries and bring to a boil. Remove from heat. Season with salt and pepper.

2. Preheat grill to medium-high. Sprinkle chicken with salt and pepper and drizzle with olive oil. Place chicken on grill and cook until juices run clear, 6-8 minutes per side. Transfer chicken to a serving platter and brush with apple-cranberry glaze.

Chicken and Turkey

Bell Pepper Chicken
Servings: 2

Ingredients
1/4 c. (7 crackers) Nabisco® Original
   Premium saltine crackers,
   finely crushed
1/2 tsp. Good Season® Garlic and
   Herb dried seasoning
2 skinless, boneless chicken breasts
2 eggs
1/2 c. each julienne red bell pepper, yellow
   bell pepper, and green bell pepper
1 small onion, cut into wedges
1 clove crushed garlic
1 1/2 c. Fleischmann's®
   Unsalted margarine
1/2 c. Kitchen's Best® Chicken stock
1/2 Tbsp. all-purpose flour
pasta for two

Instructions
1. Prepare pasta according to package directions; drain and transfer to a heated deep serving dish.

2. In a shallow dish or bowl, mix together cracker crumbs and seasoning. Crack eggs and place in separate dish or bowl, mix eggs until blended. Dip each chicken breast in egg, then coat with cracker mixture. Set aside.

3. In a large skillet sauté bell peppers, onion and garlic in margarine over medium heat until lightly crisp and tender. Remove pepper mixture from skillet and set aside; keep warm. In the same skillet, sauté coated chicken breasts in remaining margarine until browned on both sides. Remove browned chicken breasts from skillet and keep warm.

4. Combine chicken stock and flour and mix together. Pour broth mixture into pan drippings and heat through until mixture thickens and begins to boil. Stir in bell pepper mixture and heat through, stirring together.

5. Serve by placing chicken breast on bed of hot cooked pasta, pour bell pepper mixture over top.

Saucy Chicken
Servings: 4

Ingredients
4 skinless, boneless chicken breast halves - pounded to 1/2-inch thickness
2 tsp. Mrs. Dash® Original seasoning salt
6 slices Oscar Mayer® Low Sodium bacon, cut in half
1/2 c. prepared mustard
1/2 c. honey
1/4 c. light corn syrup
1/4 c. Kraft® Mayo
1 Tbsp. dried onion flakes
1 Tbsp. vegetable oil
1 c. sliced fresh mushrooms
2 Tbsp. chopped fresh parsley

Instructions
1. Rub chicken breasts with seasoning salt, cover and refrigerate for 30 minutes.

2. Preheat oven to 350°F. Place bacon in large, deep skillet. Cook over medium high heat until crisp. Set aside. In a medium bowl, combine mustard, honey, corn syrup, mayonnaise and dried onion flakes. Remove half of sauce, cover and refrigerate to serve later.

3. Heat oil in a large skillet over medium heat. Place chicken in skillet and sauté for 3-5 minutes per side, or until browned. Remove from skillet and place chicken into a 9x13-inch baking dish. Apply honey mustard sauce to each chicken breast, layer each breast with mushrooms and bacon. Bake in preheated oven for 15 minutes, or until chicken juices run clear. Garnish with parsley and serve with reserved honey mustard sauce.

Chicken and Turkey

Kathy's Chicken

Servings: 4

Ingredients

1 onion, sliced
1 Tbsp. olive oil
1 1/2 lb. skinless, boneless chicken
   tenders, or 4 chicken breasts
1- 16 oz. bottle Wishbone®
   Russian dressing
1- 20 oz. jar low sugar apricot preserve
   Smuckers® jelly
4 c. Kraft® Minute white or brown rice

Instruction

1. In skillet heat oil; place sliced onion and sauté until soft. Place chicken in 9x13-inch baking dish. In a bowl combine sliced onions, dressing and jelly and pour over chicken. If time permits, marinate in refrigerator for a few hours.

2. Bake uncovered in a 350°F oven for 1 hour. Serve over rice. Pour any extra sauce over each dish.

Braised Chicken with Herbs and Shallots

The aroma of the herbs simmering will delight your family.
Servings: 4

Ingredients

4 chicken thighs
1/2 c. all-purpose flour
2 Tbsp. olive oil
6 shallots, coarsely chopped
3 garlic cloves, crushed
1/4 c. Kitchen's Best® chicken stock
2 Tbsp. balsamic vinegar
1 1/2 c. Kitchen's Best® chicken stock
2 tsp. dried rosemary, crushed
1 tsp. crushed dried thyme
1 tsp. dried basil
1 tsp. dried marjoram
1/4 tsp. salt
1/8 tsp. ground black pepper

Instructions

1. Preheat oven to 350°F. Place chicken in flour to coat. Heat oil in a large skillet. Add shallots; sauté until browned. Add chicken and cook on each side, about 2 minutes per side. Add garlic and sauté for 1 minute. Add 1/4 c. chicken stock and vinegar and boil until liquid is reduced by half, 2 - 3 minutes.

2. Add remaining chicken stock, rosemary, thyme, basil, marjoram, salt and pepper. Bring to a boil. Cover and bake 20 - 30 minutes, or until chicken is tender.

Chicken and Turkey

Lemon Chicken
Servings: 3

Ingredients
1/4 c. olive oil
4 garlic cloves, minced
2 c. plum tomatoes, chopped
1/2 c. white cooking wine
1/4 c. lemon juice from concentrate
1/2 tsp. sugar
1 onion, chopped
3 chicken breasts
1/8 tsp. red pepper flakes
1 Tbsp. basil

Instructions
In a large skillet cook chicken with garlic and olive oil until chicken is no longer pink inside, about 7 minutes. Add tomatoes, onions and red pepper flakes; cook for 5 minutes. Pour in cooking wine, lemon juice, basil and sugar; simmer for 6 minutes. Serve with a side of white rice or toss with fettuccini.

Chicken Stuffed Green Peppers
Servings: 4

Ingredients
4 large green peppers
1/3 c. chopped onion
1 garlic clove, minced
2 Tbsp. Fleischmann's® Unsalted butter
    or margarine
3 c. diced cooked chicken
2 c. Swansons® 100% fat free
    chicken broth
2 c. Kraft® Minute Maid® brown rice
1/3 c. sliced celery
1/4 c. chopped carrots
1/4 tsp. dried basil
1/4 tsp. dried thyme
1- 4 1/2 oz. can diced tomatoes,
    undrained
1 c. fresh mushrooms
1/2 c. chopped zucchini

Instructions
1. Cut tops off of green peppers; remove seeds. In a large pot cook peppers in boiling water for 3 minutes, drain and rinse in cold water; set aside.

2. In a skillet sauté onions and garlic in butter until tender. Add chicken, broth, rice, celery, carrots, basil and thyme; bring to a boil. Reduce heat. Stir in tomatoes, mushrooms and zucchini; cover and let simmer for 25 minutes.

3. Generously fill each greeen pepper with mixture, serve hot.

Chicken and Turkey

Herbed Turkey Breast

*Herbs tucked under the skin give the turkey
a wonderful aroma as its roasting.*
Servings: 12

Ingredients
8 1/2 lbs. bone-in turkey
2 Tbsp. and 3/4 tsp. lemon juice, divided
1 Tbsp. and 1 1/2 tsp. olive oil, divided
1 1/2 garlic cloves, minced
1/4 tsp. sage
3/4 tsp. grated lemon peel
3/4 tsp. dried thyme
1 tsp. salt
1/2 tsp. pepper

Instructions
1. Loosen skin from turkey with fingers, leaving skin attached along bottom edges. In a small bowl, combine 1 Tbsp. lemon juice, 1 Tbsp. olive oil, garlic, sage, lemon peel, thyme, salt and pepper. Spread under turkey skin. Combine remaining lemon juice and oil; set aside.

2. Place turkey on rack in shallow roasting pan. Bake, uncovered, in a 350°F oven for 2 1/2 - 3 hours or until a meat thermometer reads 170°F; baste every 15-20 minutes with lemon mixture. Let stand for 10 minutes. Discard skin before carving.

Shrimp Jambalaya

Servings: 5

Ingredients

2 c. shrimp
3 Tbsp. Fleischmann's®
　　Unsalted margarine
1 c. onion, sliced
1 c. uncooked Kraft® Minute white rice
1/4 tsp. garlic powder
3/4 c. green pepper, diced
1 1/2 c. white wine or 2 Tbsp. sugar
1- 28 oz. can chopped tomatoes
1/2 tsp. thyme
1/4 tsp. basil
1/4 tsp. marjoram
1/4 tsp. paprika
1/4 tsp. hot pepper sauce
1 tsp. salt

Instructions

Sauté onion, garlic and diced green pepper in margarine until onions are tender and lightly gold. Add tomatoes, wine, salt, hot pepper sauce, herbs and shrimp; mix well. Bring to a boil. Add rice gradually stirring constantly, cover and reduce heat. Simmer for 25 minutes.

Oven-Roasted Shrimp with Salsa

Servings: 6

Ingredients

1/2 lb. Roma tomatoes, diced
1 onion, peeled and diced
2 limes, juiced
1 jalapeño chili, seeded and minced
1/2 tsp. ground cumin
1 1/2 lbs. large shrimp, peeled
　　and de-veined
2 Tbsp. olive oil
1/2 tsp. salt
1/4 tsp. ground black pepper

Instructions

1. Preheat oven to 450°F. In a 13x9x2-inch baking dish, combine tomatoes, onion, lime juice, jalapeño and cumin; mix well.

2. Toss shrimp with olive oil, salt and pepper. Evenly spread out shrimp atop tomato mixture. Place in oven and cook until shrimp are pink and salsa is hot, about 8 minutes. Turn halfway through to ensure even cooking. Serve warm.

Seafood

Grilled Orange, Shrimp and Vegetable Skewers

Servings: 4

Ingredients
1 c. olive oil
2 tsp. garlic, minced
2 tsp. finely grated lemon peel
1 tsp. finely grated orange peel
1 tsp. red pepper flakes
2 oranges, cut into small wedges
1/2 lb. large shrimp, cleaned
    and de-veined
1/2 red bell pepper, cut into 1-inch chunks
1/2 red onion, cut into 1-inch chunks
1/8 tsp. salt

Instructions
1. Whisk together oil, garlic, lemon peels, orange peels, and red pepper flakes in a small bowl. Thread skewers as follows: orange wedge, shrimp, pepper and onion, and end with another orange wedge. Place skewers in container with marinade and chill 2 1/2 hours, spooning occasionally with marinade.

2. To cook, preheat broiler or grill. Cook skewers, turning frequently and brushing with marinade, until shrimp are pink all over, about 5 minutes. Season with salt and serve.

Sautéed Cajun-Style Tuna

Servings: 3

Ingredients
1 lb. tuna steak
1 tsp. paprika
1/4 tsp. of each ground black pepper,
    ground cumin, cayenne pepper,
    dried thyme, dried oregano and
    dried basil
1 Tbsp. minced peeled onion
1/2 tsp. garlic, minced
1 lemon, juiced
1 Tbsp. distilled white vinegar
1/8 tsp. salt
2 Tbsp. fresh parsley, chopped
1 lime, cut into wedges

Instructions
1. Rinse tuna, drain and set aside. In a small bowl, combine paprika, pepper, cumin, cayenne, thyme, oregano and basil. Heat skillet on medium. Add spice mixture and toast, stirring constantly, for 30-50 seconds.

2. Add onions and garlic and cook, stirring constantly, 1 minute. Add tuna, lemon juice, vinegar and salt. Cover, reduce heat to low and cook 3 minutes. Turn tuna over and cook for another 5 minutes or until tuna is tender. Raise heat to reduce some of the liquid. Transfer to serving plate and spoon on spicy juices. Serve with parsley and a lime wedge.

Seafood

Baked Halibut in White Wine and Herbs
Servings: 4

Ingredients
4- 6 oz. halibut steaks
1/2 tsp. salt
1/4 tsp. ground black pepper
1/4 c. dry white wine
2 Tbsp. lemon juice
1 Tbsp. olive oil
2 green onions, minced
2 garlic cloves, peeled and minced
1 tsp. crushed dried oregano

Instructions
Preheat oven to 400°F. Season halibut on both sides with salt and pepper. Place in a single layer in baking dish. Whisk together wine, lemon juice, olive oil, green onions, garlic and oregano. Pour over halibut, cover and bake for 20 minutes, or until done. Halibut should flake easily with a fork. Serve immediately.

Grilled Salmon
Servings: 4

Ingredients
6- 6 oz. salmon fillets, skin on
3 Tbsp. extra virgin olive oil, divided
1 1/2 c. Zesta® Original saltine crackers, finely crushed
3 Tbsp. fresh Italian parsley, chopped
1 garlic clove, minced
1 tsp. finely grated lemon peel
1 tsp. finely grated orange peel
1 tsp. salt, divided
1 tsp. ground black pepper, divided

Instructions
1. Preheat grill. In a large skillet, heat 2 Tbsp. oil over medium heat. Add crushed crackers and sauté for 3 minutes, or until crackers are toasted. Transfer to a small bowl and stir in parsley, garlic, lemon peel, orange peel, 1/4 tsp. salt and 1/4 tsp. pepper; set aside.

2. Lightly oil grill. Brush salmon with remaining oil and season with remaining salt and pepper. Place salmon, skin side up on grill. Grill 4-5 minutes on each side or until it flakes easily with a fork. Transfer to serving plates, sprinkle with mixture and serve.

Pasta

Mike's Specialty Pasta

My brother-in-laws special pasta recipe.
Servings: 4

Ingredients

1- 28 oz. can chopped and
    peeled tomatoes
4 Tbsp. olive oil
1 medium onion, finely chopped
4 garlic cloves, minced
1 Tbsp. Reese® anchovy paste
2 tsp. hot pepper flakes
pinch of ground coriander seed
1- 16 oz. package penne noodles

Instructions

1. Prepare pasta according to package directions; drain and transfer to a heated, deep serving dish.

2. Meanwhile, sauté tomatoes over medium heat. Add olive oil, onions, and garlic; sauté for 5 minutes. Add anchovy paste and pepper flakes. Simmer for 30-40 minutes. Add coriander. Place mixture over cooked noodles.

Summer Penne alla Puttanesca

A superb pasta dish. Serve with a loaf of French bread.
Servings: 8

Ingredients

1 lb. plum tomatoes, seeded and diced
24 black olives, pitted and halved
4 shallots, peeled and chopped
2 Tbsp. olive oil
1/4 c. fresh basil leaves, coarsely chopped
1/4 tsp. salt
1/8 tsp. ground black pepper
1/2 Tbsp. dried chilies, crushed
1/2 c. virgin olive oil
16 oz. penne pasta

Instructions

1. In a medium bowl, combine tomatoes, olives, shallots, oil and basil; mix well. Season to taste with salt, pepper and chilies. Pour enough olive oil over tomato mixture to coat; set aside.

2. Prepare pasta according to package directions, drain and transfer to a heated deep serving dish. Add marinated vegetable mixture and toss to heat.

Pasta with Maple Mustard Chicken

Servings: 4

Ingredients

1/4 c. and 2 Tbsp. olive oil, divided
1 garlic clove, minced
1 Tbsp. rosemary, chopped
1 Tbsp. chives, chopped
1 Tbsp. apple cider vinegar
2 1/2 Tbsp. maple syrup
2 Tbsp. Dijon style mustard
3 Skinless boneless chicken breasts
1 c. Kitchen's Best® chicken stock
3/4 c. roasted red peppers, diced
1/4 c. sun-dried tomatoes, chopped
1/4 lb. snow peas, stemmed and
    lightly steamed
1/2 lb. penne pasta

Instructions

1. Prepare pasta according to package directions, drain and transfer to a heated deep serving dish.

2. In a large skillet over medium heat sauté garlic in 2 Tbsp. olive oil for 30 seconds. Add herbs and vinegar and cook 30 seconds more. Pour mixture into small bowl to cool; whisk in maple syrup and mustard. Place chicken in a glass baking dish and pour in marinade. Turn once to coat. Cover bowl and chill chicken for at least one hour.

3. Heat remaining oil in a large skillet over medium high-heat. Meanwhile, remove chicken from glass dish, saving marinade and sprinkle it with salt and pepper. Add chicken to skillet and sauté for 2 minutes on each side to seal in juices. Reduce heat to medium and continue heating chicken until cooked, about 6 minutes. Transfer chicken to cutting board and cut into bite-size cubes.

4. Deglaze pan by adding 1/2 c. chicken stock to skillet and simmer until stock reduces by half. Add remaining stock and reserved marinade and bring mixture to a boil. Continue cooking at a simmer until liquid has thickened, 5 more minutes.

5. Combine chicken cubes, roasted red peppers, sun-dried tomatoes, snow peas and cooked pasta in a large bowl. Pour in sauce and toss pasta to combine. Season to taste with salt and pepper.

Pasta

Marinated Tomatoes in Vermicelli

Servings: 8

Ingredients
10 tomatoes, sliced
1/2 c. olive oil
2 garlic gloves, minced
1/2 c. black olives, sliced
1 tsp. dried basil, crushed
1/8 tsp. salt
1 lb. package vermicelli

Instructions
1. Toss tomatoes with olive oil; add garlic, black olives, basil and salt. Refrigerate for 2 hours.

2. Before serving prepare vermicelli according to package directions; drain. Add marinated tomatoes and toss until coated evenly.

Pasta with Chicken Cacciatore Sauce

Servings: 8

Ingredients
1- 16 oz. package spaghetti
2 Tbsp. olive oil
1 lb. boneless, skinless chicken breasts, cut into 1-inch pieces
2 onions, peeled and chopped
3 garlic cloves, peeled and minced
2 c. mushrooms, sliced
1- 28 oz. can plum tomatoes, with juice
2/3 c. dry red wine
1 green pepper, seeded and thinly sliced
1/4 c. trimmed and minced parsley
1 tsp. crushed dried oregano
1/2 tsp. crushed dried thyme
1 bay leaf

Instructions
1. Prepare pasta according to package directions; drain and transfer to a heated, deep serving dish.

2. Heat oil in a large skillet over medium-high heat. Add chicken and sauté until lightly browned, 5 - 8 minutes. Remove pieces to plate with slotted spoon; reserve pan drippings.

3. Add to skillet onions and garlic, sauté in pan drippings over medium heat for 3 minutes. Add mushrooms and sauté for 6 minutes. Add tomatoes, wine, sautéed chicken, green pepper, parsley, oregano, thyme and bay leaf. Simmer gently for 25 - 30 minutes. Let stand for 5 minutes to allow sauce to thicken. Serve over hot spaghetti.

Pasta

Lemon Shrimp Pasta
Servings: 4

Ingredients
1/2 lb. dried angel hair pasta
3 Tbsp. olive oil
3 garlic cloves, peeled and minced
2- 14.5 oz. can diced tomatoes, drained
1 lemon, juiced
1 Tbsp. fresh oregano, chopped
1/8 tsp. salt
1/8 tsp. ground black pepper
1 lb. shrimp, peeled and de-veined
1 lemon, sliced in 1/4-inch slices

Instructions
1. Cook pasta according to package directions; drain and set aside.

2. In a large skillet heat oil; add garlic and sauté until golden, about 1 minute. Add tomatoes, oregano, lemon juice, salt and pepper. Lower heat and simmer for 5 minutes. Add shrimp and cook until just pink. Add pasta and toss until thoroughly heated. Serve hot.

Light Shrimp Scampi
Servings: 4

Ingredients
8 oz. angel hair pasta
2 Tbsp. olive oil
4 garlic cloves, peeled and minced
1 lb. shrimp, shelled and de-veined
1 c. Kitchen's Best® fish stock
1/2 c. dry white wine
1/4 c. fresh parsley, minced
4 tsp. lemon peel, finely grated
2 tsp. Cream® cornstarch
1/4 c. lemon juice
1/8 tsp. ground black pepper

Instructions
1. Cook pasta according to package directions; drain. Meanwhile, in a large skillet, heat oil and sauté garlic over medium heat. When garlic sizzles, add shrimp and sauté just until shrimp turns pink, about 1 minute. Stir in fish stock, wine, parsley and lemon peel.

2. In a small bowl, stir cornstarch with lemon juice until cornstarch dissolves, then whisk into shrimp mixture. Simmer until sauce begins to thicken slightly, about 1 minute. Serve over pasta and season generously with black pepper.

Pasta

Spaghetti and Meatballs with Marinara Sauce

Servings: 4

Ingredients

8 meatballs – see recipe on page 6
8 to 12 oz. dried spaghetti, linguine,
    or other pasta
1 c. fresh mushrooms, sliced
3/4 c. onions, chopped
2 garlic cloves, minced
1 Tbsp. olive oil
4 c. chopped, peeled tomatoes (6 large),
    or 2- 14 1/2 oz. can tomatoes cut up
1- 6 oz. can tomato paste
2 Tbsp. fresh parsley, snipped
2 tsp. Good Season® Garlic and Herb
    dried seasoning
1 tsp. sugar
1/4 tsp. ground black pepper

Instructions

1. Make meatballs according to recipe on page 6.

2. Prepare pasta according to package directions, drain and transfer to a heated deep serving dish.

3. Meanwhile, in a large pot, cook mushrooms, onions and garlic in hot oil until onions are tender. Stir in tomatoes, tomato paste, parsley, seasoning, sugar and pepper. Bring to a boil; reduce heat. Cover and simmer for 30 minutes, stirring once or twice. Serve over cooked pasta.

Sun-dried Penne Pasta

Servings: 6

Ingredients

8 oz. pkg. penne pasta
1- 4 oz. bottle Kraft® Zesty
    Italian Dressing
1 c. chopped tomato (1 large tomato)
3 1/2 oz. jar sun-dried tomatoes in oil,
    drained and chopped
1/4 c. chopped fresh parsley

Instructions

Cook pasta according to package directions, drain. Combine dressing, tomatoes and parsley then mix in cooked pasta. Refrigerate for several hours or overnight. Serve hot or cold.

Sweet Endings

The Culinary Guide for MSPI

Sweet Endings

Pies

Mini Cherry Pies

These mini fruit pies are fun to make especially with little ones.
Servings: (2) 4- inch pies

Ingredients

1 c. all-purpose flour
1 Tbsp. sugar
1/2 tsp. salt
6 Tbsp. Fleischmann's®
    Unsalted margarine

Pie Filling:
1- 16 oz. canned sour cherries
1/2 tsp. cinnamon
1/8 tsp. nutmeg
1 Tbsp. lemon juice
2 tsp. cornstarch

Instructions

1. To make dough combine flour, sugar, and salt in a large bowl. Cut margarine into flour until mixture resembles coarse meal.

2. Add up to 3 Tbsp. ice water and mix until just combined. Wrap in plastic wrap and chill for 30 minutes.

3. Preheat oven to 350°F. Divide dough into 4 sections and roll each out to a 1/8-inch thickness.

4. Line (2) 4-inch pie plates each with a piece of rolled dough. In a medium bowl combine cherry filling, cinnamon, nutmeg, lemon juice and cornstarch, divide evenly between the two dough pieces.

5. With a mini cookie cutter cut vents in the remaining two dough pieces and drape each over the pies. Crimp the edges to seal and bake until filling is bubbling and crust is golden 50-60 minutes.

Apple Cranberry Pie

A sweet tart taste given from both the apples and cranberries, distinguishes this pie from the classic apple pie.
Servings: 8

Ingredients

1 Pillsbury® refrigerated pie crust
2 c. apples, peeled, cored and quartered
2 c. fresh cranberries
2/3 c. sugar
1 Tbsp. lemon juice
1 1/2 Tbsp. all-purpose flour

Crumb Topping:
1/2 c. all-purpose flour
1/2 c. sugar
1/4 tsp. cinnamon
4 Tbsp. Fleischmann's® Unsalted
     margarine, cut into 1/4-inch pieces

Instruction

1. Heat oven to 400°F. Line a 9-inch pie pan with pastry, fluting edges. Thinly slice apples crosswise and combine in a large bowl with cranberries. Add sugar, lemon juice and flour, mixing well. Transfer filling to a pie shell, smoothing top of fruit. Bake for 30 minutes.

2. Meanwhile, in a large bowl, mix flour, sugar and cinnamon for topping. Add butter, mixing it into dry ingredients until mixture resembles coarse crumbs.

3. After 30 minutes, remove pie from the oven and reduce temperature to 375°F. Spread crumb topping over pie and bake for another 25 - 30 minutes, until top is golden and fruit thickens and bubbles around edges. Cool pie for 2 hours before serving.

Pies

To Die for Blueberry Pie

The name says it all.
Servings: 8

Ingredients
1 Pillsbury® refrigerated pie crust
2 pints fresh blueberries (5 cups)
1 tsp. grated lemon peel
1/2 tsp. ground cinnamon
1/2 c. and 2 tsp. sugar
1/3 c. all-purpose flour
1 Tbsp. Fleischmann's®
    Unsalted margarine

Instructions
1. Gently toss blueberries, lemon peel, cinnamon, 1/2 c. sugar and flour. Spoon mixture into crust. Cut margarine into small pieces; sprinkle on top of blueberry mixture. Preheat oven to 425°F.

2. Place one dough crust on bottom of a 9-inch pie plate. Place blueberry mixture on top of crust. Top with the second dough crust. Sprinkle top of pie with remaining 2 tsp. sugar. Bake 40 minutes.

Rosy Raspberry Pie

Servings: 8

Ingredients
1 Pillsbury® refrigerated pie crust
3 c. fresh raspberries
1 c. sugar
3 Tbsp. Cream® cornstarch
1 c. water
2 Tbsp. Kayro® corn syrup
2 Tbsp. raspberry-flavored gelatin

Instructions
1. Gently wash raspberries with water and drain. In a medium saucepan, combine sugar and cornstarch. Stir in water and corn syrup. Cook and stir over medium heat until thick and bubbly. Stir in gelatin. Cook and stir for 2 minutes more. Remove mixture from heat. Cover surface with plastic wrap and let cook for 30 minutes.

2. Meanwhile, preheat oven to 375°F. Bake pie crust for 15 minutes. Place raspberries in an even layer in bottom of pie crust. Pour cooled gelatin mixture over raspberries. Cover and chill 3 hours or until gelatin is set.

Lemon Meringue Pie

Servings: 8

Ingredients

1 Pillsbury® refrigerated pie crust

Pie Filling:
1/4 c. Cream® corn starch
1 c. sugar
1/4 c. lemon juice
3 egg yolks
1 1/2 c. water
1 tsp. grated lemon rind
1 Tbsp. Fleischmann's®
    Unsalted margarine

Meringue:
3 egg whites
6 Tbsp. sugar

Instructions

1. Prepare pie crust according to package directions.

2. In a medium saucepan, combine corn starch, sugar and lemon juice; mix well. Beat egg yolks; add to corn starch mixture. Add water. Stirring constantly, bring mixture just to a boil over medium heat and simmer gently for 5 minutes. Remove from heat. Add margarine and grated lemon rind to thickened mixture and stir until thoroughly blended. Pour into baked pie shell.

3. Preheat oven to 400°F. With mixer at high speed, beat egg whites until soft peaks form. Gradually add sugar. Continue to beat on high speed to form stiff, glossy peaks. Spread meringue over filling. Bake for 9 minutes or until golden. Cool on rack away from draft for 2 hours. Refrigerate; serve cold.

Bars

Frosted Banana Bars

Servings: 16 bars

Ingredients

1/2 c. Fleischmann's® Unsalted margarine
2 c. sugar
3 eggs
1 tsp. vanilla extract
2 c. all-purpose flour
1 tsp. baking soda
1/2 c. bananas, mashed

Instructions

1. In a medium bowl cream butter and sugar. Beat in eggs, bananas and vanilla. In a small bowl combine flour, baking soda and salt; add to creamed mixture and mix well.

2. Pour into greased 9x13-inch pan and bake in a 350°F oven for 25 minutes.

Raspberry Streusel Bars

Servings: 12

Ingredients

1 1/4 c. Quaker® quick oats, uncooked
1 1/4 c. all-purpose flour
1/2 c. firmly packed brown sugar
1 tsp. baking powder
1/4 tsp. salt
1 3/4 stick Fleischmann's® Unsalted margarine
1 c. raspberry jam
3/4 c. Tops® Real Semi-Sweet Chocolate Chips

Instructions

1. Preheat oven to 350°F. In a large bowl combine oats, flour, brown sugar, baking powder and salt. Stir in margarine until mixture is crumbly.

2. Reserve 1 c. crumb mixture; set aside. Press remaining crumb mixture into bottom of an 8-inch square pan. Bake 10 minutes.

3. Spread raspberry fruit evenly over baked crust to within 1/4-inch of edges. Sprinkle with 1/2 c. chocolate chips.

4. Combine reserved crumb mixture with remaining 1/4 c. chocolate chips. Sprinkle over fruit mixture, pressing lightly into fruit. Bake 30-35 minutes or until golden brown.

5. Cool completely on wire rack before cutting into squares.

Chunky Pecan Pie Bars

One of Eric's favorite pies is pecan pie. This is a new twist to a sweet dessert that we all can enjoy.
Servings: 12 bars

Ingredients
1 1/2 c. all-purpose flour
1/2 c. Fleischmann's® Unsalted margarine
1/4 c. brown sugar

Filling:
3 large eggs
3/4 c. Karo® light corn syrup
3/4 c. granulated sugar
2 Tbsp. Fleischmann's®
    Unsalted margarine
1 tsp. vanilla extract
1 3/4 c. Tops® Real Semi-Sweet
    Chocolate Chips
1 1/2 c. chopped pecans (optional)

Instructions
Heat oven to 350°F. Grease a 9x13-inch pan. In a small bowl beat with an electric mixer flour, margarine and brown sugar until crumbly. Press into pan and bake for 20 minutes.

Filling:
Whisk eggs, corn syrup, granulated sugar, butter and vanilla. Stir in chocolate chips and nuts. Pour over baked crust. Bake in a 350°F oven for 25-30 minutes.

Chewy Homemade Granola Bars

Servings: 16 rectangular bars

Ingredients
1/2 c. Fleischmann's® Unsalted margarine
1/3 c. sugar
1/3 c. honey
1/4 c. all-purpose flour
1/2 tsp. vanilla extract
1/4 tsp. cinnamon
2 c. Kellogs® Rice Krispies® cereal
2 c. rolled Quaker® oats
1 c. Tops® Real Semi-Sweet
    Chocolate Chips

Instructions
1. Heat oven to 350°F. Coat a 9x13-inch pan. Melt margarine. Remove from burner and whisk in sugar, honey, flour, vanilla extract and cinnamon. Add remaining ingredients and mix well. Transfer mixture to pan.

2. Using a sheet of waxed paper and palm of hand, press granola firmly into pan. Bake for 20 minutes. Cool for 1 hour then cut into rectangular bars.

Bars

S'Mores

Servings: 16

Ingredients
1 package Nabisco® Graham
    original crackers
2 1/2 c. Sam's Choice™ Real Semi-Sweet
    Chocolate, chocolate chips
1- 10 oz. bag large or small marshmallows

Instructions
1. Preheat oven to 350°F. On an ungreased cookie sheet, place one layer graham crackers seams together. Top with 2 c. chocolate chips, followed by marshmallows.

2. Cook in oven 7 minutes or until marshmallows have melted. Remove from oven; with spatula spread marshmallows. Sprinkle with remaining 1/2 c. chocolate chips. Serve warm.

Just a Kracker

Servings: 2 dozen

Ingredients
1 ream of Saltine® crackers or Nabisco®
    Grahams- honey
1 c. Fleischmann's® Unsalted margarine
3/4 c. brown sugar
2 c. Tops® Real Semi-Sweet
    Chocolate Chips
3/4 c. walnuts or pecans (optional)

Instructions
Lay crackers on cookie sheet. Boil butter and brown sugar. Pour over crackers and bake for 5 minutes in a 400°F oven. Pour chocolate chips on top and let stand for 1 minute then spread with spatula. Top with nuts. Let cool and cut into chunks.

Rice Krispies® Treats

Always a favorite and so easy to make.
Servings: 24 squares

Ingredients
6 c. Kellogs® Rice Krispies® cereal
3 Tbsp. Fleischmann's®
    Unsalted margarine
1- 10 oz. bag regular marshmallows

Instructions
1. Melt margarine in saucepan on low heat. Add marshmallows and stir until marshmallows are melted. Remove from heat, add cereal and stir until well coated.

2. Using a buttered spatula, press mixture evenly into a greased 9x13-inch pan. When cooled, cut into 2-inch squares.

Cakes

Double Layer Birthday Cake
Servings: 8-12 slices

Ingredients
3 c. Pillsbury® Softasilk® cake flour
1 3/4 c. sugar
1 1/4 c. water
1/2 c. shortening
2 eggs
2 1/2 tsp. baking powder
1 tsp. salt
1 1/2 tsp. vanilla extract

Instructions
1. Preheat oven to 350°F. Grease and flour two cake pans. In a large bowl, combine all ingredients.

2. Using an electric mixer, beat until well mixed, approximately 4 minutes. Pour batter into cake pans. Bake for 40-45 minutes or until a toothpick inserted in center comes out clean.

3. Cool in pans 10 minutes before removing to wire racks. Frost when completely cooled. Choose from one of the listed frostings on page 109.

Note: Duncan Hines® makes several cake, frosting and brownie mixes without milk and soy protein.

Heavenly Chocolate Cupcakes
Servings: 12

Ingredients
2 c. sugar
1 c. Hersheys® Unsweetened cocoa
1 c. Fleischmann's® Unsalted margarine
2 c. water
3 Tbsp. oil
3 Tbsp. water
2 tsp. each of baking powder and
    baking soda
1/2 tsp. salt
1 tsp. vanilla extract
4 c. all-purpose flour

Instructions
1. Preheat oven to 400°F. Line muffin tins with paper liners. Set aside. In a large bowl, combine everything but the flour. Beat until well mixed. Stir in flour and mix well.

2. Fill muffin tins 2/3 full. Bake 18 minutes or until toothpick inserted in center comes out clean. Remove to wire rack to cool before frosting.

Frostings

Minty Frosting

Servings: 2- 8-inch cakes; 1- 13x9-inch cake; 36 cupcakes

Ingredients
2 c. confectioner's sugar
1/2 c. Fleischmann's® Unsalted
    margarine, softened
1/2 tsp. salt
1 Tbsp. water
1/2 tsp. vanilla extract
1/4 tsp. mint extract

Instructions
In a small bowl, combine sugar, margarine, salt, water and vanilla and mint extracts. Beat until light and fluffy.

Cocoa Frosting

Servings: 2- 8-inch cakes; 1- 13x9-inch cake; 36 cupcakes

Ingredients
1/2 c. Fleischmann's® Unsalted margarine
1/2 c. Hershey's® Unsweetened
    Cocoa powder
2 2/3 c. confectioner's sugar
1/4 c. water
1 tsp. vanilla extract

Instructions
In a large mixing bowl beat margarine on medium speed until softened, about 1 minute. Add remaining ingredients. Beat on low speed until ingredients are moist. Beat on medium speed until creamy.

Vanilla Silk Frosting

Servings: 2- 8-inch cakes; 1- 13x9-inch cake; 36 cupcakes

Ingredients
3 c. confectioner's sugar
1/2 c. Fleischmann's® Unsalted
    margarine, softened
3 Tbsp. water
1 tsp. vanilla extract

Instructions
In a large bowl, combine all ingredients. Mix until smooth.

Note: Add a few drops of food coloring to tint frosting.

Old Fashioned Sugar Cookies

For the Thanksgiving holiday we travel to Manitowoc, Wisconsin to visit my parents. During our visit in 2003, my daughter Megan, who was 2 1/2 at the time, helped Oma make these cookies.
Servings: 1 dozen

Ingredients
1/2 c. Fleischmann's® Unsalted margarine
1 c. sugar
1 tsp. vanilla
1/4 tsp. baking soda
1/2 tsp. cream of tartar (this is a spice)
1/2 c. Crisco® shortening
1 egg
2 c. flour
1/4 tsp. salt

Instructions
1. Cream together margarine, shortening and sugar. Add 1 unbeaten egg and vanilla. Mix well. Sift and gradually add flour, baking soda, cream of tartar and salt. Chill for 3 hours.

2. Shape into balls the size of a walnut. Flatten with glass dipped in sugar. Decorate as desired and place on a cookie sheet. Bake in a 350°F oven for 10-12 minutes.

Note: You may also roll out dough and cut with cookie cutter shapes. Bake in a 375°F oven for 7-8 minutes, or until lightly golden.

Raspberry Chocolate Chip Cookies
Servings: 1 dozen

Ingredients
3 egg whites
1/8 tsp. salt
3 1/2 Tbsp. raspberry JELL-O®
3/4 c. sugar
1 tsp. white vinegar
1 c. Tops® Real Semi-Sweet
    Chocolate Chips

Instructions
1. Beat egg whites and salt until foamy. Gradually add JELL-O® and sugar; beat until peaks form. Mix in vinegar and fold in chocolate chips by hand.

2. Drop on lightly greased cookie sheet. Bake in a 250°F oven for 25 minutes.

3. Turn off oven and keep cookies inside for an additional 20 minutes.

Cookies

Classic Chocolate Chip Cookies

Be prepared, these chocolate chip cookies will disappear in minutes.
Servings: 3 dozen

Ingredients
1 c. Fleischmann's® Unsalted margarine
3/4 c. brown sugar
1/2 c. white sugar
2 tsp. vanilla
1 egg
2 1/4 c. all-purpose flour
1/2 tsp. sea salt
1 tsp. baking soda
1- 12 oz. Tops® Real Semi-Sweet
    Chocolate Chips

Instructions
1. Preheat oven to 375°F. In a small mixing bowl, combine flour, baking soda and sea salt.

3. In a large mixing bowl, cream margarine, brown and white sugars together until light and fluffy. Add vanilla and egg. Beat well. Add dry mixture to creamed mixture and mix well. Add chocolate chips and mix well. Spoon a tablespoon of dough into a ball and place on ungreased cookie sheet.

4. Bake for 11 minutes. Remove from oven and place cookies on cooling rack.

Pie Crust Cookies

Serve with a cup of coffee or hot tea.
Servings: 12 to 18 cookies

Ingredients
3/4 c. minus 2 Tbsp. all-purpose flour
1/3 tsp. salt
1/4 c. Crisco® shortening, chilled
    for 1 hour
2 Tbsp. cold water
3 Tbsp. softened Fleischmann's®
    Unsalted margarine
2 Tbsp. sugar
2 Tbsp. ground cinnamon

Instructions
1. Preheat oven to 425°F. With a fork, mix flour, salt and Crisco® until crumbly. Add water, stirring with fork until ball forms and pulls away from sides of bowl. Flour rolling surface and rolling pin. Roll out dough to 1/8-inch thickness. Spread with soft margarine, sprinkle with sugar and cinnamon. Starting at one side, roll crust into a log. Using a table knife, cut into 1-inch pieces.

2. Place cut side down on ungreased cookie sheet. Bake for 15 minutes or until lightly golden on top. Cool at least 10 minutes.

Soft Ginger Cookies

Servings: 2 dozen

Ingredients

1/4 c. Fleischmann's® Unsalted margarine
1/2 c. sugar
1 egg
1/2 tsp. baking soda
1/2 Tbsp. water
1/2 c. Grandma's® Robust or
    Original molasses
2 c. all-purpose flour
1/2 tsp. ginger

Frosting:
2 1/2 c. confectioner's sugar
1 Tbsp. Karo® white corn syrup
2 Tbsp. Fleischmann's® Unsalted
    margarine
3-4 Tbsp. hot water

Instructions

1. Cream together margarine and sugar until light and fluffy. Add egg and beat well.

2. Combine baking soda and water and add to creamed mixture. Blend in molasses. Sift together flour and ginger and gradually add to creamed mixture.

3. Drop dough by tablespoon onto greased baking sheet. Bake in a 350°F oven for 12-15 minutes. Cool before frosting.

4. To prepare frosting blend all ingredients together and spread on cooled cookies.

Specialty Desserts

Schaum Torte
Servings: 7

Ingredients
3 egg whites
1 c. sugar
1 1/2 tsp. vinegar
1/2 tsp. vanilla extract
1 pt. fresh strawberries

Instructions
1. Sprinkle egg whites with salt and whip until very dry. Gradually add sugar and beat until stiff peaks form. With a spatula fold in vinegar and vanilla. With a large spoon, drop meringue in 7 large clumps (about 4-inches in diameter). Indent the center of each torte with the back of a spoon.

2. Grease and flour cookie sheet. Bake tortes in a 225°F oven for 1 hour. Use bottom rack of stove. Turn oven off after baking for 1 hour and keep in for an additional 10 minutes. Serve with fresh strawberries.

Lemon Meringue Kisses

Servings: 12

Ingredients

3 eggs, separated
1/4 tsp. cream of tartar (this is a spice)
1 pinch salt
1/2 c. sugar
1/2 tsp. lemon extract

Instructions

1. Preheat oven to 200°F. Combine egg whites, cream of tartar and salt in a medium bowl. Beat with an electric mixer on medium speed until foamy. Gradually add sugar, beating on high until stiff and glossy. Fold in lemon extract.

2. Line cookie sheet with parchment paper. Spoon 12-inch circle shape mounds of egg white mixture onto baking sheet; each should be approximately 3 inches across. Using the back of a spoon, round out the center of each meringue mound to form a cup.

3. Bake for 1 hour or until shells lift off the paper easily. Transfer to wire rack to cool completely.

Specialty Desserts

Oranges in Grand Marnier®

Servings: 6

Ingredients
6 Tbsp. finely sliced orange peel,
   colored part only
1/2 c. water
6 oranges
1 c. water
1/4 c. sugar
2 Tbsp. Karo® light corn syrup
1/4 c. Grand Marnier® or any type
   of brandy
2 Tbsp. lemon juice

Instructions
1. In a small saucepan, combine orange peel and water. Bring to a boil, drain and set aside.

2. Using a sharp knife, cut off as much peel and pith from oranges as possible. Slice oranges crosswise and arrange overlapping on a platter.

3. Combine water, sugar and corn syrup in saucepan; bring to a boil, stirring only until sugar has dissolved. Add orange peel and simmer, uncovered, for 25 minutes or until syrup is slightly thick. Remove from heat. Stir in brandy and lemon juice. Cool slightly and pour over oranges. Refrigerate for 2 hours, turning oranges twice.

French Apple Cobbler

Servings: 4

Ingredients
6 apples, peeled, cored and diced
1/2 c. all-purpose flour
1/2 c. granulated sugar
1 Tbsp. cinnamon
1 large egg, lightly beaten
2 Tbsp. Fleischmann's® Unsalted
   margarine or butter
1/2 tsp. baking powder
1/8 tsp. salt

Instructions
1. Preheat oven to 350°F. Place apples in a 9-inch square baking pan. Mix flour, sugar, egg, margarine, baking powder and salt in a medium bowl until blended.

2. Drop dough by heaping tablespoons over scalloped apples. Bake for 25-30 minutes or until apples are tender and crust is golden brown.

Infants with a history of cow's milk protein intolerance have a greater risk of developing soy protein intolerance. The intestinal mucosa damaged by cow's milk protein may allow increased uptake of the potentially allergenic soy protein.[13]

The
Culinary Guide
for MSPI

Calcium Requirements

Milk and other dairy products are a major source of nutrients in the American diet. The most important of these nutrients is calcium. Calcium is essential for the growth and repair of bones throughout life. In the middle and later years, a shortage of calcium may lead to thin, fragile bones that break easily, a condition called osteoporosis.

In 1997, the Institute of Medicine released a report recommending new requirements for daily calcium intake. The amount of calcium a person needs to maintain good health varies by age group. Recommendations from the report are shown in the following table.[14]

Age group	Amount of calcium to consume daily, in milligrams (mg)
0-6 months	210 mg
7-12 months	270 mg
1-3 years	500 mg
4-8 years	800 mg
9-18 years	1,300 mg
19-50 years	1,000 mg
51-70+ years	1,200 mg

Without milk in the diet how can nutritional needs of the body be met? Excellent sources of calcium include green vegetables (broccoli, collard greens, turnip greens, and kale), fish with soft, edible bones (salmon and sardines), and seafood (oysters and shrimp). Calcium can not be absorbed without Vitamin D. Sources of Vitamin D include eggs, liver, and sunlight.[15]

A supplemental vitamin may also be helpful. However, vitamins, even those with extra calcium, generally only have about 200 mg, or 20% of daily requirements. Supplementing these vitamins with foods labeled 'High in Calcium' may be needed.[16]

Resources

Glossary of Ingredients to Avoid

Casein and Caseinates: Casein and caseinates are used as extenders and tenderizers in imitation sausages, leaves, soups and stews.

Curd: When it coagulates, milk separates into a semisolid portion (curd) and a watery liquid, whey. Cheese is made from the curd.

Custard: A pudding like dessert (made with a sweetened mixture of milk and eggs) that can either be baked or stirred on stovetop.

Ghee: A liquid butter, used especially in the cooking of India, made from the milk of cows or buffaloes and clarified by boiling.

Hydrolysates (casein, milk protein, protein, whey, whey protein): Hydrolyzed proteins are used in a variety of food, pharmaceutical, nutritional, and personal care products, where binding, emulsification, and film forming functionalities are required.

Lactalbumin: An albumin that is obtained from whey and is similar to serum albumin.

Lactoglobulin: The globulin present in milk.

Lactose: Is the sugars found in milk including breast milk.

Whey: The watery material which remains after most of the protein and fat have been removed from milk.

Miso: Miso is a basic flavoring in much of Japanese cooking. Miso is used in sauces, soups, marinades, dips, main dishes, salad dressings and as a table condiment.

Shoyu sauce: A Japanese term. A brown liquid sauce made by subjecting beans (as soybeans) to long fermentation and to digestion in brine.

Soy protein (concentrate, isolate): Proteins which are present in or isolated from soybeans.

Tamari: A thick sauce made from soybeans (similar to soy sauce).

Tempeh: A fermented soybean cake, with a texture similar to that of soft tofu and a yeasty, nutty flavor.

Tofu: Also known as soybean curd and bean curd. White tofu is made from curdled soy milk.

How to Read an Ingredient Label

Below are three sample food labels found on packaged food products. Note how carefully labels must be read. There is no consistency to where products indicate a milk and/or soy product.

INGREDIENTS: WATER, MUSHROOMS, VEGETABLE OIL (CORN, COTTONSEED, CANOLA AND/OR SOYBEAN), MODIFIED FOOD STARCH, WHEAT FLOUR, CREAM, CONTAINS LESS THAN 2% OF THE FOLLOWING INGREDIENTS: SALT, DRIED WHEY, MONOSODIUM GLUTAMATE, SOY PROTEIN CONCENTRATE, DRIED DAIRY BLEND (WHEY, CALCIUM CASEINATE), YEAST EXTRACT, SPICE EXTRACT, DEHYDRATED GARLIC.
CAMPBELL SOUP COMPANY, CAMDEN, NJ, U.S.A. 08103-1701

Label one indicates a milk and soy protein ingredient in the 4th and 5th lines. 4th line: DRIED WHEY, SOY PROTEIN. 5th line: DRIED DAIRY BLEND (WHEY, CALCIUM CASEINATE).

INGREDIENTS: SUGAR, WATER, PARTIALLY HYDROGENATED VEGETABLE OIL (SOYBEAN AND COTTONSEED OILS), CORN SYRUP, COCOA PROCESSED WITH ALKALI, CORN STARCH, MONO- AND DIGLYCERIDES, NON-FAT MILK, SALT, CREAM, POLYSORBATE 60, POTASSIUM SORBATE (PRESERVATIVE), CITRIC ACID, SODIUM ACID PYROPHOS-PHATE, SODIUM CITRATE, SOY LECITHIN, NATURAL AND ARTIFICIAL FLAVORS.
CONTAINS MILK.
DISTRIBUTED BY: AURORA FOODS INC.
11432 LACKLAND ROAD
ST. LOUIS, MO 63146 USA
FROSTS TWO 8" OR 9" LAYERS OR A 13" X 9" CAKE, BROWNIES OR ABOUT 36 CUPCAKES
DIRECTIONS FOR EASY SPREADING FROSTING
• Store unopened can at room temperature, not over 90°F.
• Stir room temperature frosting in can before using (cold frosting is difficult to spread).
• Cool cake completely. Brush loose crumbs off cake before frosting.
• Cover and refrigerate any remaining frosting for up to 2 weeks.

65-00439-06

Label two indicates that this product does contain a milk ingredient. Many companies are moving to place common allergy ingredients in bold as shown below.

*Percent Daily Values are based on a 2,000 calorie diet.
INGREDIENTS: SOYBEAN OIL, WATER, EGGS, VINEGAR, CONTAINS LESS THAN 2% OF EGG YOLKS, LEMON JUICE CONCENTRATE, SALT, SUGAR, DRIED ONIONS, DRIED GARLIC, PA-PRIKA, NATURAL FLAVOR, CALCIUM DISODI-UM EDTA (TO PROTECT FLAVOR)
KRAFT FOODS NORTH AMERICA, INC.
GLENVIEW, IL 60025 USA   (B002A)
© KF HOLDINGS
KRAFT
kraftfoods.com
real help in real time ™
1.800.847.1997
se habla español
04000814500900

Label three is safe for someone with MSPI to consume. Soybean oil is not a soy protein ingredient.

Resources

Weights and Measures

3 teaspoons	=	1 tablespoon	1 cup	=	pint
2 tablespoons	=	1/8 cup	2 cups	=	1 pint
4 tablespoons	=	1/4 cup	4 cups	=	1 quart
5 1/3 tablespoons	=	1/3 cup	4 quarts	=	1 gallon
8 tablespoons	=	1/2 cup	8 quarts	=	1 peck
10 2/3 tablespoons	=	2/3 cup	4 pecks	=	1 bushel
12 tablespoons	=	3/4 cup	1 liter	=	2.1 pints
16 tablespoons	=	1 cup	1 kilogram	=	2.2 pounds
1 cup	=	8 fluid ounces	28.3 grams	=	1 ounce

Equivalent Chart

1 small to medium onion	=	1 cup chopped
4 stalks celery	=	1 cup
28 saltine crackers	=	1 cup crumbs
14 square graham crackers	=	1 cup crumbs
1 lemon	=	3 Tbsp. juice
1 orange	=	1/2 cup juice
4 egg whites	=	1/2 cup

Conversion of Fahrenheit and Centigrade

To convert Fahrenheit into Centigrade: subtract 32, multiply by 5, divide by 9
Ex. 100°F − 32 = 68; 68 x 5 = 340; 340 ÷ 9 = 38°C

To convert Centigrade into Fahrenheit: multiply by 9, divide by 5, add 32
Ex. 100°C x 9 = 900; 900 ÷ 5 = 180; 180 + 32 = 212°F

Oven Temperature

Fahrenheit	Centigrade	Gas mark	Description
225 F°	110 C°	1/4	very cool
250 F°	130 C°	1/2	
275 F°	140 C°	1	cool
300 F°	150 C°	2	
325 F°	160 C°	3	very moderate
350 F°	180 C°	4	moderate
375 F°	190 C°	5	
400 F°	200 C°	6	moderately hot
425 F°	220 C°	7	hot
450 F°	230 C°	8	
475 F°	240 C°	9	very hot

Resources

Index

Resources

Resources

Resources

References

[1] Cobb, Albert Jr., MD. "Babies and Food Allergies." <u>Allergy and Family Medicine</u>. 2003 http://www.allergyclinicsanmarcus.com/baby_foodallergies.html.

[2] E - mail from mspiguide.com.

[3] "Food Intolerance." <u>Food Standards Agency</u>. ‹http://www.foodstandards.gov.uk/health-iereating/allergyintol/›.

[4] E - mail from mspiguide.com.

[5] E - mail from mspiguide.com.

[6] "Intolerance Versus Allergy." <u>Allergic Reactions and Anaphylaxis Information from the Distributor of EpiPen® Epinephrine Auto-Injectors</u>. 2003 DEY.

[7] Iannelli, Vincent, MD. "Kids and Food Allergies" <u>What You Need to Know About Pediatrics</u>. About, Inc.2004. ‹http://pediatrics.about.com/cs/nutrition/a/food_allergies.htm›.

[8] "Lactose Intolerance." <u>National Digestive Diseases Information Clearinghouse (NDDIC)</u>. NIH Publication No. 03-2757 March 2003. ‹http://digestive.niddk.nih.gov/ddiseases/pubs/lacto-seintolerance/index.htm›.

[9] "Tips for Managing a Milk Allergy" <u>The Food Allergy & Anaphylaxis Network</u>. ‹http://www.Foodallergy.org›.

[10] "What is soy lecithin? Is it safe for a soy-allergic individual?" Featured Topic. <u>Food Allergy News</u>:2: 1, 2001‹http://www.foodallergy.org/topics_archive/lecithin.html›.

[11] "Tips for Managing a Milk Allergy" <u>The Food Allergy & Anaphylaxis Network</u> ‹http://www.Foodallergy.org›.

[12] Falci, Kenneth J., Ph.D., Gombas, Kathy L., Elliot, Elisa L., Ph.D. "Food Allergen Awareness: An FDA Priority." <u>U.S. Food and Drug Administration. Center for Food and Applied Nutrition</u>. Reprinted from Food Safety Magazine Feb-March 2001 issue. August 28, 2001 ‹http://www.cfsan.fda.gov/~dms/alrgawar.html›.

[13] Guandalini, Stefano, MD., Nocerine, Agostino, MD. "Soy Protein Intolerance." <u>eMedicine</u>. April 18, 2003.2004, eMedicine.com, Inc. ‹http://www.emedicine.com/ped/topic2128.htm›.

Resources

[14] "Lactose Intolerance." <u>National Digestive Diseases Information Clearinghouse (NDDIC)</u>. NIH Publication No. 03-2757 March 2003. ‹http://digestive.niddk.nih.gov/ddiseases/pubs/lactoseintolerance/index.htm›.

[15] Tidwell, Judy. "Milk Allergy." <u>What You Need to Know About Allergies</u>. About, Inc. 2004 ‹http://allergies.about.com/cs/milk/a/aa082399.htm›.

[16] Iannelli, Vincent, MD. "Toddler Milk and Calcium Requirements" <u>What You Need to Know About Pediatrics</u>. About, Inc. 2004 ‹http://pediatrics.about.com/cs/weeklyquestion/a/020602_ask.htm›.

About the Author

Jane and her family live in Avon, Ohio. Jane earned bachelor degrees in public communications from Ashland University and hearing and speech science from Ohio University. She has a master's degree in higher education administration from The University of Akron and holds a secondary education teaching certificate. Jane also earned CTM status as a member of Toastmasters International.

Jane resigned from Myers College as Director of Parma Heights and Brecksville Academic Centers to stay home with her two children, Megan and Pieter. During the summer months she teaches tennis at The EMH Center for Health & Fitness in Avon, OH.

Any questions or comments regarding this publication, please send e-mail to jane@mspicookbook.com.